WE COULD BE HEROES

ISBN 978-2-36568-093-6

WE COULD BE HEROES

RAPHAËL BARONTINI

PATRICK CHAMOISEAU
CHERYL FINLEY
MIKE LADD

JBE BOOKS

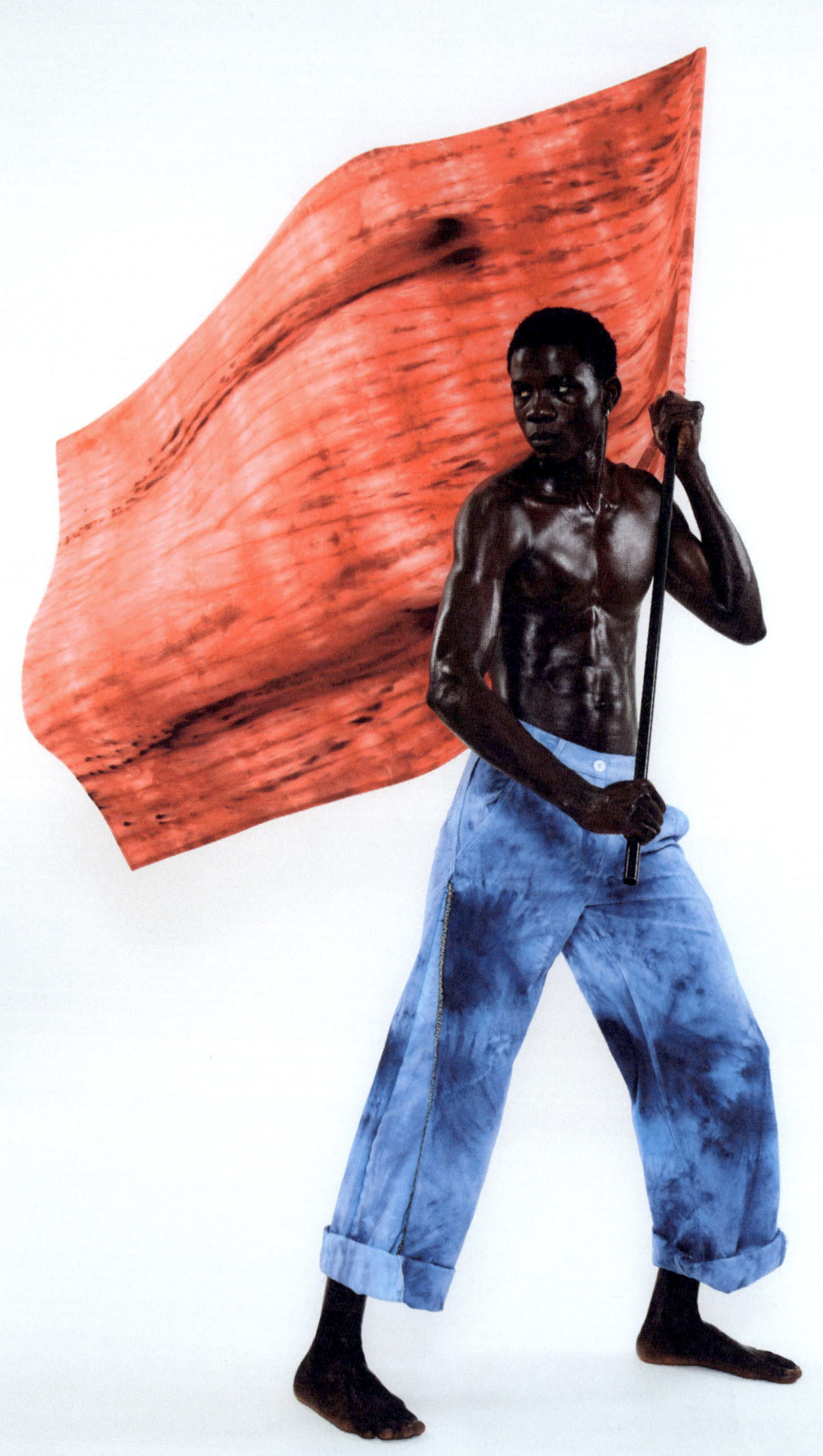

PANTHÉON OF RELATION

PATRICK CHAMOISEAU

The plantation system in the West Indies and the Americas was the laboratory for what we are living through today. During the 17th and 18th centuries, Western slave ships transported millions of men, women and children towards this enslavement machine that was quite distinct from ancient forms of slavery. The latter still left their victims with a connection, however bleak, to their humanity. In contrast, American-style slavery consisted of an almost ontological dehumanization of an entire portion of humanity, on the sole basis of a fiction—a true narrative damnation—which created the "Negro": subhuman, avatar of the word "slave," consubstantial with the savagery invented for Africa. The millions of African captives who arrived alive to these plantations, both on the islands and the mainland, escaped an abyss that within a few centuries would swallow millions of their companions in misfortune—those who could not bear the unthinkable hardship of the crossing. This colossal maritime mausoleum is still referred to by its seemingly innocuous Western toponym: the Atlantic Ocean. Édouard Glissant, in his new vision of the world, associated it with those in the slave ship's hold, and together they cried out its name: *The Abyss*!

The survivors of the Abyss weren't simply obligated to resist the servile damnation inflicted upon them—they had to recover their very humanity. They worked at it in classical ways (the First and Second Maroon Wars) which gave us (after the great Native Americans who rose up against their genocide) the very first Afro-Creole-American heroes: the *Maroons*—majesties without thrones or statues, existing beneath the consciousness of the world. Yet, opposition to the plantation system forged divergent, profound and radical paths as well: paths of creativity. What the mechanisms of domination, whatever they may be, strip from their victims is, above all, their ability to create—to soften or blur the reality of enslavement through Deleuzian lines of flight, unforeseen prospects, deconstructions of the deadly "reality" through murmurs brought back from the unfathomable of the "Real." For this we need powerful artists… which brings us to Raphaël Barontini.

Homo sapiens is an inventor of the world. Inhabiting a demiurgic imagination distinguishes the sapiens from the animal without them ceasing to be one—in this way humans construct a thousand little "realities" that their minds create, which allow them to escape the unthinkable horrors of the "Real." An escape that is unattainable—its exact perception remains uninhabitable, even terrifying, unless one becomes a sorcerer, a shaman, a poet, or embodies the poetic brazenness of an artist. To reoxygenate our realities, the artist makes excursions into the "Real" and returns with living configurations of materials, *forms* and *forces*, epiphanic visions, which set our entire mind in motion, renewing in this way—often from the ground up—our reality. Today, unlike ancient times, our artists go there without magic, without mysticism, but with just the spirit of science and technique, logos, and the cognitive galaxies of the poetic. The slaveholders were keen to this power: they very quickly banned those they had damned from employing even the subtlest sign, symbol, sculpture, effigy, statuette, assemblage or indecipherable shape, which could potentially be part of some allegorical projection, and thus a recourse to ancient orishas, a sort of obscured Oya, likely to stir up a surge of revolt. The tools, utensils, partitions of the huts, and clothes worn by the enslaved remained bare, stripped of any inscription, color, sign, design… A nudity of the absence imposed on oneself. As a result, visual arts would make an unexpected extension in our places…

Our first resistance fighters, even before the Maroons, were the artists. The inaugural creator was the one who, in the hold of the boat, managed to swallow their tongue, or to throw themself over the protective netting, into the sacrificial mouth of the sharks—thus combining, in a devastating performance, death and life, decision and renunciation, consuming them together at high intensity in a cardinal negation of all enslavement. The second creator was the sorcerer. They would employ their knowledge of plants to poison the master's cattle, his domestic slaves, and, on occasion, the master himself. They would conjure the reigning dark forces into small forms in which various improbable elements combined to produce power. Even today we encounter these small "quimbois" (small sculptured charms called as such) at the crossroads of our misfortunes and our hopes. However, these creations existed in the shadows, were never claimed or signed, never openly worn, haunting the night, inhabiting the "sacred wound" of which Aimé Césaire spoke; they were not equated into the global agenda against which waves of Maroons were constantly thrusted...
Yet the subsequent creators found the solution.

In these sinister plantations, the most resolute creativity was, in fact, ambiguous. To be adopted by the greatest number of those aspiring to rehumanization, the creations had to be accepted by the master. This required them to be integrated, in one way or another, into the obsessive preoccupation of the slavers: the production of sugar, tobacco, cotton, and other shitty products ensuring their fortune. Dancing, drumming, singing, and of course the elocution of primordial storytellers, were woven into the workshops, accompanied the work in the fields, adapted to the chains. Nevertheless, these creative veins blossomed like midnight flowers in the places where the enslaved could gather for themselves.[1] The masters had noticed that these practices appeased the mood of their captives, dissipated their heavy melancholy, reduced suicides and apparently brought more enthusiasm to collective work. Despite everything, an unsuspected dimension infiltrated. In these assemblies,

1. These gatherings always took place at night, on Sundays or holidays, with circles of participants spread out around a center where the creators intervened. The Creole language calls these circles "*Lawond*," "*La-ronde*." The *Lawonds* are multifaceted: mortuary vigil or an evening of Bèlè in Martinique, Léwoz in Guadeloupe, Maloya in Réunion, Candomblé in Brazil, Santeria in Cuba, Voodoo in Haiti, Mayolè in Marie Galante, Quadrille Balls almost everywhere...

led by the improvised artists (very singular individuals, all creators of themselves and creators of others), mysterious revelations of another possible existence would occur. Dancing, drumming, singing, and storytelling are at once individual and collective arts, in mutually generative ensembles. The work of art creates the one who receives it, who prolongs and diffuses it through the fruitfulness of their reception of it, and in this way creates it in return. It is through this alchemy that "nations" would appear, historical singularities to which two or three of the various ancestors of Raphaël Barontini certainly belonged.

During their nighttime assemblies, the enslaved first adopted the strategy of gathering by "nation"—*nasyon* in Creole. Slave owners applied this term to people of the same ethnic group or African origin. Usually, slaveholders were careful to mix people together in order to avoid concentrations that would be conducive to the dreaded revolts. But, in the long run, they eventually allowed groupings of "nations" based on the good behavior of certain peoples—those who appeared the most docile, who would upkeep their gardens, were hardworking, who did not commit suicide "over nothing" or excelled despite whatever difficulty... This meant that in certain places, groupings of ethnic groups occurred—fortuitous, partial, favoring the survival of a handful of wisdoms carried over from a lost land, from a missing humanity. Those who saw themselves gathered like this formed a "nation," like shipwrecked people clinging to a floating object. However the term would very quickly expand. Whether you were of African birth (Bossale) or were Creole (born on the plantation), or even whether you were of mixed race descended from unexpected mixtures, one found oneself faced with the same dehumanization, estrangement from the world, that had to be resisted by the underground creation of another world. The "nations" therefore became open congregations.
They practiced common dances, songs well connected to each other, specific tales, culinary practices, they cultivated special techniques and chosen beliefs. They got together for evenings, vigils, events and seemingly innocent social rituals. They thus weaved existential structures, and outlined, in the very middle

of the plantation, an architecture of oblique meanings and values that the slaveholders could not perceive. The "nations" appointed themselves kings, queens, viceroys, vicequeens, ladies-in-waiting, squires, treasurer and flag bearers, masters of ceremonies and guardians of offices, with a flight of dignitaries (Governor-*this*, Consul-*if-you-will*, Captain-*that*, Marshall-*nice-blouse*...). Dressed in spectacular costumes, they adorned themselves in the trappings of the colonial powers: crowns, decrees, flags, braids, seals, insignia, hats, which appeared to the masters as mimetic attestations of submission. They referred to each other in such innocuous ways the slavers could only welcome it: names of Christian saints, flowers but also colors (Rose, Garnet, Violet...), underneath which were hidden martial designations or guised valor. Whereas slaveholders saw it only as mere operetta theatrics, feeding their own imaginations, the "nation" was a forum for narcissistic restoration and a majestic proclamation of humanity. It established mutual aid between the enslaved people for all stages of existence, accompanying births, marriages, and baptisms with brilliance and style, instituting social significance and relational networks, enlivening emotions foreign to plantation life, and above all: accompanying death.

When your life is stolen, you at least want control over your death. Everyone dreaded being buried haphazardly anywhere, whatever way, like a toad, without a beautiful lace garment, without a coffin, without even a grain of dignity, in some razed corner. The "nations" offered burials (usually hasty and desolate), and a cheerful ceremony, with dances, rhythms, songs, stories, official saints, authorized prayers, and loads of old, invisible forces. With the earnings from their resourcefulness, the members of a "nation" would contribute to tontines, bit by bit, penny by penny, which fueled the functioning of the group. And so, these organizations would serve as a generic matrix for the first mutualist societies, mutual aid societies, and other brotherhoods of cooperation, which were the basis for the trade unions and political parties in our countries. They would also be the unsuspected foundations of the Maroon revolts (starting in Martinique with the revolt of May 22, 1848) which, stitch by stitch, tore away at the official suppressions. And this is where we get even closer to Raphaël Barontini: these "nations" did not miss any opportunity to appear in broad daylight—to present themselves with sharp and high standards. Release the "*convoys*"! Or in Creole, the "*konvwa*"!...

The "nations" marched in fervent procession at even the slightest religious occasion. However, the ideal circumstance was Carnival. The settlers practiced it in their villages and cities, in their own way, with little wolves on their eyes, Venetian disguises, precious costumes and powdery makeup. The "nations" arrived there in "convoys," processions imbued with ironic gravity, baroque solemnity, or in the joyful parades that the Creole language calls "*vidés*" or *emptied*. Adorned in ceremonial costumes, the kings, queens and extravagant series of dignitaries displayed their signs, insignias, banners, flags, canvases, colors, tattoos, shoes, stockings, English embroidery, collars and splendid laces... Their bodies were living canvases, standing banners, dancing sculptures that in Africa or Asia animate divine masks. Their very skins, adorned with vegetal hues, jewels, bracelets and necklaces were bases for creation. Each one created and recreated themself, beneath an indecipherable role which they performed with what smiling solemnity, cunning grace, vain decency, crazy pride and wild will can contain projecting joy. Europe in its diversity mixed with African and pre-Columbian presences, religious symbols that had fallen from the buccaneer ships so far from their ports, abandoned colors of all pallets spurned unprecedented intoxications. A rainbow of multiple symbolizations, linked to flowers, materials, repurposed objects, with refrains, cavalcades, recounted declarations... an excessive pomp in which the colonists saw nothing but grotesque, quirky, good-natured joy, but which, we now know, imposed on them a *determined humanity*.

One of the characteristics of the plantation system is that it was the primer, not only of the global capitalist regime that would plunge the globe into economic gehenna, but of a general state of shock. Cultures, civilizations, languages, gods, their imaginations, signs and symbols, were thrown into a maelstrom of fluidity and vertebral forces that Glissant would call: *Tout-monde* (All-world, or the world in its entirety). Everything is connected to everything. By shock, violence and domination, but also by secret circulations (fermentations, hybridizations, unpredictable mixtures, marvels of the composite, links between antagonists)—a creolization by which individuals will be freed from the monolithic envelopment of the old communities. Édouard Glissant would name this unpredictable fluidity: *the Relation*. The world over, these individuations would find themselves (like our creators in the sumptuous convoys) without any existential ready-to-wear models, with only the exhortation to create themselves, one by one, alone, improvising a meaning to their own existence, precipitated onto the neverending ladder of the interconnected world. They will be forced to solitarily invent new solidarities, not through community fusions, but on the relational basis of an "I," creator, creative, committed and conscious, developing a foliage of "we" (shared dreams, ideals, struggles, utopias and potential follies). In a "convoy" of enslaved Black people, there might be Native Americans or even some poor white folks. Women could hold eminent positions. All were integrated into the processions and found themselves reborn into the collective intention. The "convoys" went beyond the sole level of resistance to envisage, beyond a solidarity of the dominated, the mobilization of a general meeting where everything could (on the basis of the parade, the song, the dance, the word, the sign and the symbol) be reborn, move forward, pulse lines of flight, recompose the world, live the world—where everything could enter into Relation.

I smile at the idea that the old Panthéon, asleep in its icy darkness, hesitating between the house of the gods, the church and the tomb; transfixed in its function of celebrating national history by wielding a large ax; excluding other stories, memories, the junctions of our diversities from its initial project; closed in by its narrow celebration of great men, to which the people, even less so the women, and even less so the Black people, could never reach; apical selection, inaccessible to persistent minorities; this vertical edifice of nation, created in an exclusive logic that guards borders, thus subjecting the world to a solitary vow; having recently experienced small openings, sparingly welcoming what had not been planned, modestly honoring what had never been envisaged until then; yes, I like the idea that this time, this monument of an old world, suddenly reveals this ovation of materials, forces and forms, fabrics, leathers, rhythms and colors, this artistic "convoy" that triggers in through Raphaël Barontini. I see Barontini as the son of the *nasyon*, heir to the "convoys," a global meta-mestizo for whom the border is but the threshold of a flavor, an artist who is solitary yet in solidarity with all imaginations, who inhabits the world differently, who dreams of it differently, exercising the slogan of a collective trans-encountering that colonialism and the imperial spirit have so deeply distorted, and exercising it according to the sole credo of Beauty, to the point of transforming this age-old palace into a home—lively, sparkling, which resounds with the enthusiasm of solemnity, and the acclaim which Saint-John Perse ascribed to the highest esteem...

Raphaël, seer of chimeras, may this old monument be transformed through you in beautiful metamorphoses, may it resound—in its crypt, through its galleries, under its trinitarian dome—with a whole new world, and may it finally become—valid for all, with concern for all—a true pantheon of Relation. ◆

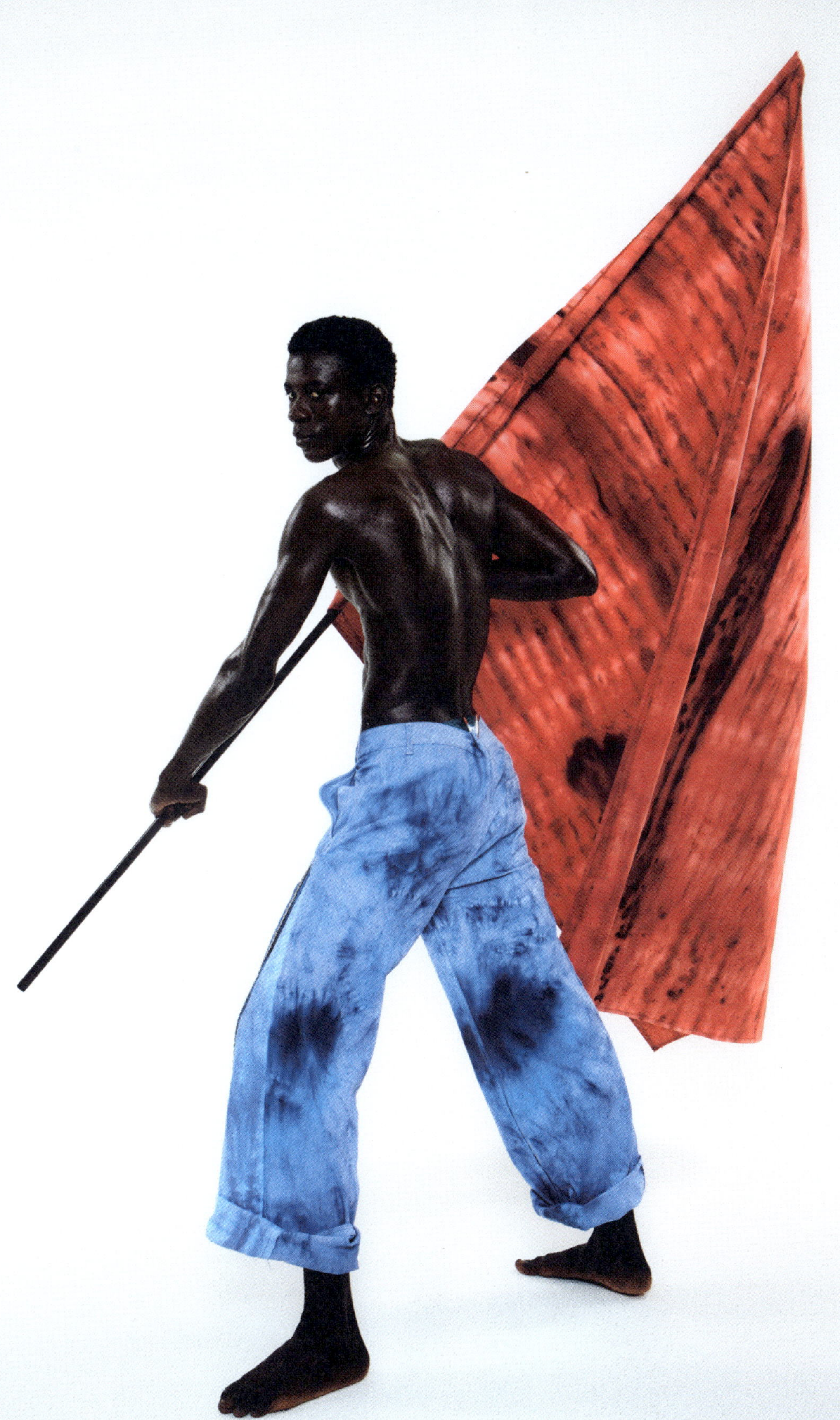

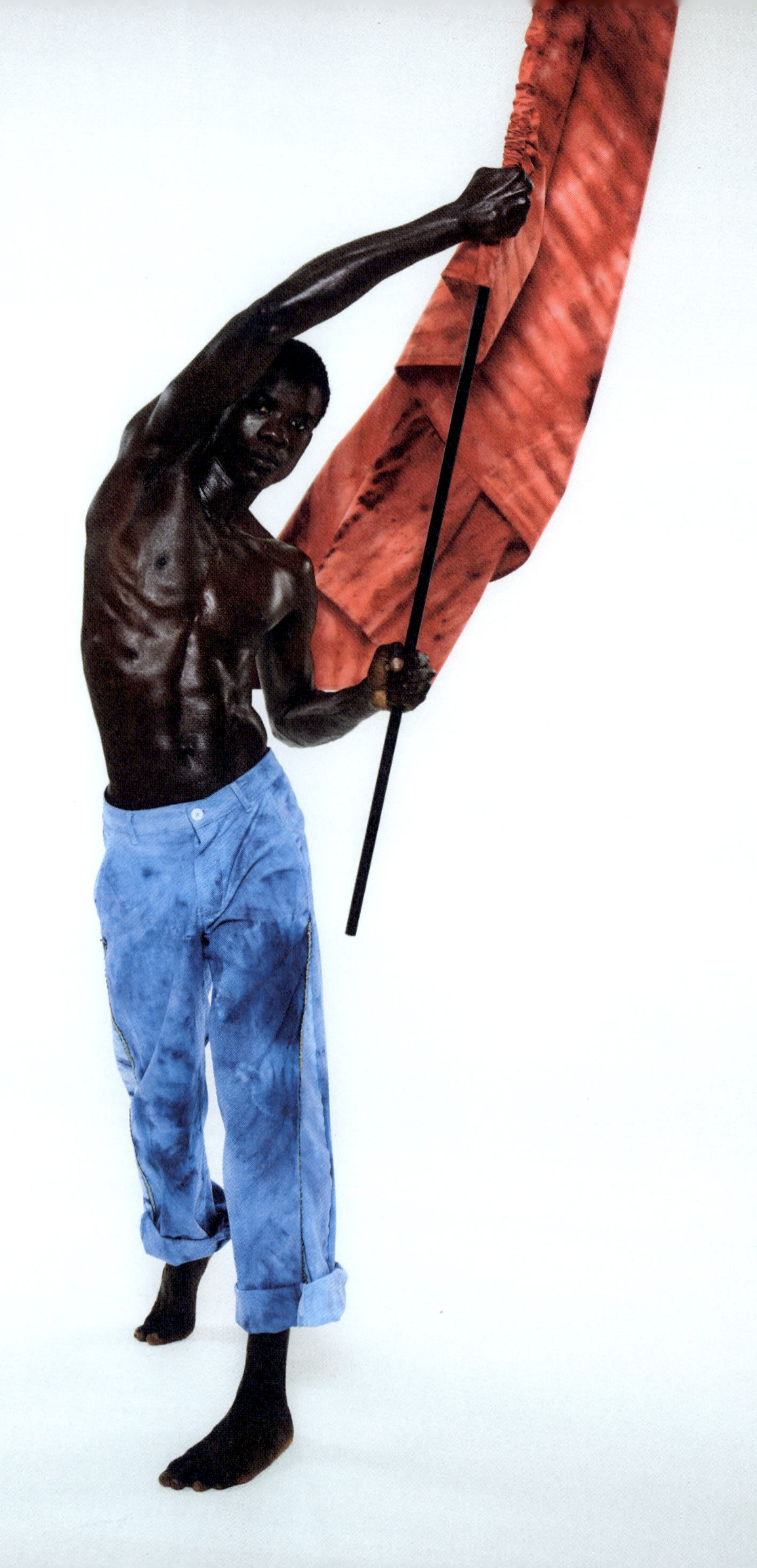

AWAKENING THE DEAD, HEALING THE NATION

CHERYL FINLEY

Raphaël Barontini leads a cadre of contemporary artists of the African diaspora who participate in what I have called a practice of mnemonic aesthetics, wherein they deploy key images, portraits, objects and iconographies of past historical narratives depicting resistance to enslavement and colonialism as a call to action for contemporary audiences to engage in ongoing struggles to be free, to effect sustainable structural change, to combat racism, xenophobia and disenfranchisement, to imagine vibrant possibilities, and bright, new futures. Among these, the image of the slave ship, portraits of revolutionary leaders, including Toussaint L'Ouverture (c. 1743-1803) or John Brown (1800-1859), and abolitionists such as Olaudah Equiano (c. 1745-1797), Nanny of the Maroons (c. 1685-1755) or Frederick Douglass (c. 1817-1895), remain standards of the arsenal and stand out in the works of these artist-activists. Barontini pays homage to some of these seminal figures and introduces imagined ones in the monumental *We Could Be Heroes* commissioned by the Center of National Monuments at the Panthéon in Paris, October 19, 2023 – February 11, 2024.

Activating images, objects and artifacts imbued with Afro-Caribbean history and lived experience, Barontini employs *mnemonic aesthetics*—a ritualized politics of remembering—and demonstrates how this key cultural practice of contemporary artists of the African and Caribbean diasporas mobilize strategies of repetition, rhythm and ritual to make hidden histories tangible and actionable, frequently employing print-based, photographic or time-based technologies. "These artists often work and rework, reimagine and reinterpret the material sources they use as a base."[1]

1. Cheryl Finley, *Committed to Memory: The Art of the Slave Ship Icon* (Princeton: Princeton University Press, 2018), p. 11. Some of the artists known for their works using mnemonic aesthetic practices include Hew Locke, Keith Piper and Ingrid Pollard in England; Hank Willis Thomas, Betye Saar and Maria Magdalena Campos-Pons in the US; Romauld Hazoume in Benin and Guy Gabon of Guadeloupe, among many others.

In Barontini's case, he seizes archival sources, artifacts, and ephemera—prints, photographs, reproductions of paintings and ritual objects—and through his multi-media practice, reinterprets, positions, cuts, reinserts and reclaims them to elevate and expose the untold and hidden histories of the Caribbean diaspora in France. Barontini's subversions of the archive act as interventions, shedding light—literally—on artifacts sequestered and confined to the archive or reinterpreting anew centuries-old history paintings and prints to propose alternatives to the colonial narrative, updating it with the stories, figures and cultural tools of Black resistance, liberation, identity, beauty and power. The practice of mnemonic aesthetics is a decolonial methodology in which artists like Barontini and others find new meaning in archival images and objects to help correct, amend and reimagine the historical record.

The Crossing is one of the two largest textile panoramas of *We Could Be Heroes*, spanning the width of the North Transept of the Panthéon, where natural light from the windows above lend a radiance and levity to the silkscreened and pieced fabrics, allowing them to glow and flow with the air currents. Featured prominently in this work is the schematic image, *Description of a Slave Ship*[A] (1789), made famous by the foundational work of Thomas Clarkson (1760–1846), the underrecognized British abolitionist instrumental in researching, theorizing, and activating the campaign for ending the transatlantic slave trade in 1807, and later chattel slavery as an institution in the British Colonies in 1833. He traveled to Paris on the eve of the French Revolution in 1789 with copies of the woodblock print, which exposed for the first time the manner in which enslaved Africans were violently and inhumanely packaged and transported across the Atlantic from West Africa to the Americas during the transatlantic slave trade. Clarkson met with members of the Société des Amis des Noirs and shared this print with statesmen Abbé Grégoire and the Comte de Mirabeau (both buried in the Panthéon), who commissioned a miniature frigate after the print with carved figures representing enslaved people. In Barontini's

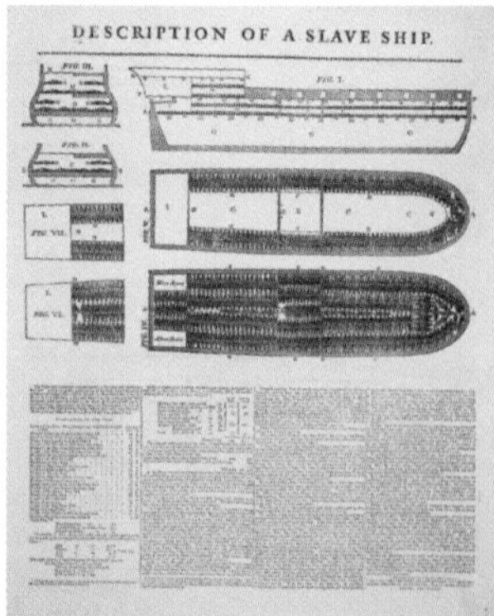

A. *Description of a Slave Ship*, 1789, 64 × 51 cm.

hands, however, 235 years later, the famous print of the slave ship is cut, excerpted, and pieced together, forming the hulls of two separate sailing vessels, driving the brutal narrative of the Middle Passage across the moving panorama. Hands and limbs reach out from the ships' hulls, while shackles hang down from the purple-hued night sky, full moon aglow. To the left on the shore is one of the oldest plantations in Guadeloupe, in Marie-Galante, and to the right, enlarged Fang masks stand watch over the sailing vessels, a reminder that religious, literary, cultural and musical practices traveled with the enslaved people to the abyss or onward to the new world. Named *The Crossing*, this panorama draws upon the seminal work of Martinican poet and theorist, Édouard Glissant (1928-2011), notably his poem, the "Open Boat," from his critically acclaimed *Poetics of Relation.*[2]

2. Édouard Glissant, *Poetics of Relation*, Betsy Wing, Translator. Ann Arbor: University of Michigan Press, 1997.

Above, closer to the windows, three additional textiles in the North Transept complement *The Crossing*, using a similar color palette of subdued blues, purples and steely grays: *The Maroon*, *Léwoz* and *The Abyss*. In *The Maroon*, Barontini depicts one of many courageous enslaved Africans who took to the mountains, dense foliage and untraveled routes to get away and self-emancipate. Resistant and determined, they developed their own societies, living apart from French planters while secretly interacting with enslaved people on plantations via social relations and the exchange of goods and services. Barontini's textile work shows a figure on the move in the early light of dawn, high up in mountains shrouded by lush greenery and comforted by a periwinkle sky. With its flat representation of verdant rushes, the sun and the figure in profile, this luminous work recalls similar panels from Jacob Lawrence's (1917-2000) *Toussaint L'Ouverture Series* (1938), where the artist used bold colors and angular, flattened perspectives to portray the life of the revolutionary leader of the Haitian Revolution. To the far right, *Léwoz* celebrates the musical and dance traditions developed on the plantations of Guadeloupe and Martinique, notably "Ka," in which the percussive sound of the drum was originally derived from animal skin-covered wooden barrels once used to transport wine, salted fish or meats, oil or rum, as enslaved people were not allowed to cut down trees. At the center, *The Abyss* brings us back to the work of Édouard Glissant and a metaphorical interpretation of the Middle Passage using the free-falling *Negro Study* of the famous nineteenth-century artist-model, Joseph[B], who was painted by the French-Haitian child prodigy, Théodore Chassériau (1819-1856), in 1838. The artist, who was born in El Limón, Santo Domingo (now Dominican Republic), migrated to France with his family and studied with Jean-Auguste-Dominique Ingres at the age of eleven, and later Eugène Delacroix, before exhibiting at the Paris Salon in 1836 at the age of seventeen. The model, Joseph, was also painted by Théodore Géricault (1791-1824), best known for the large-scale history painting, *Raft of the Medusa*, 1818-19, in which Joseph is seen at the pinnacle of the faltering raft, transporting survivors of the shipwrecked frigate Medusa, which had run aground in a storm. Géricault's painting of this controversial subject, in which all but fifteen of the one hundred forty-seven on board survived, launched his career at the Paris Salon of 1819.

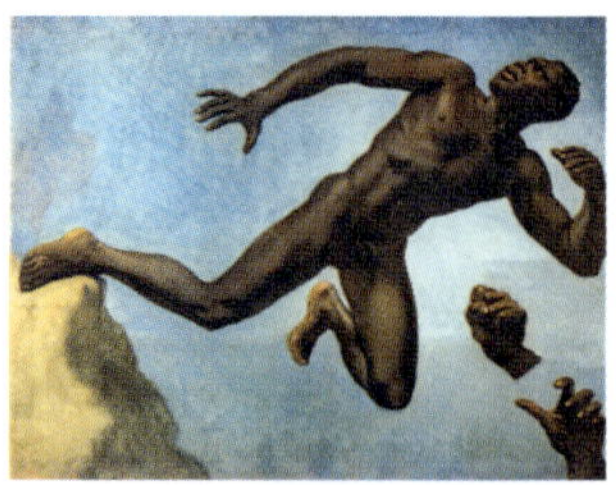

B. Théodore Chassériau, *Étude de noir d'après le modèle Joseph*, 1838, 73 × 59 cm.

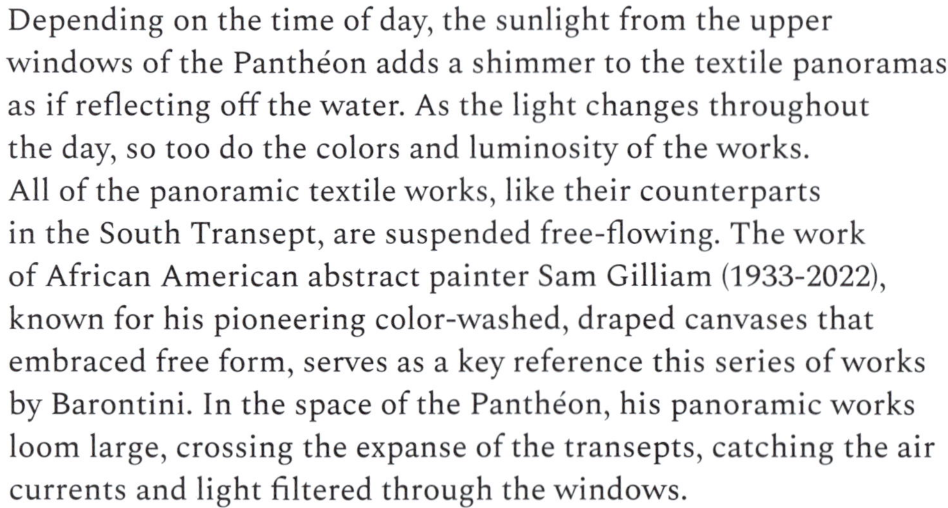

Depending on the time of day, the sunlight from the upper windows of the Panthéon adds a shimmer to the textile panoramas as if reflecting off the water. As the light changes throughout the day, so too do the colors and luminosity of the works. All of the panoramic textile works, like their counterparts in the South Transept, are suspended free-flowing. The work of African American abstract painter Sam Gilliam (1933-2022), known for his pioneering color-washed, draped canvases that embraced free form, serves as a key reference this series of works by Barontini. In the space of the Panthéon, his panoramic works loom large, crossing the expanse of the transepts, catching the air currents and light filtered through the windows.

Featured prominently in the suite of three panoramic textiles depicting the Battle of Vertières (1803) in the South Transept, *Toussaint's Triumph* highlights the figure of Toussaint L'Ouverture (1743-1803), who long has compelled artists for his seminal role in global Black resistance movements, notably in leading the Haitian Revolution (1791-1804), resulting in the first independent Black nation in Latin America. For example, renowned African American artist, Jacob Lawrence, pioneered his signature historical narrative style of "dynamic cubism," painting flat figures with bold colors, as early as 1938 at the age of twenty-one with the *Toussaint L'Ouverture Series* of forty-one gouache paintings, which Harlem Renaissance philosopher, Alain Locke (1885-1954), called "one of the most important" and "symbolic" works of the time.[3] For that series, the young Lawrence conducted detailed research at the 135th Street branch of the New York Public Library (now the Schomburg Center for Research in Black Culture) to craft captions and images that chronicled specific moments in the years-long struggle, and studied with Harlem Renaissance artists Augusta Savage (1892-1962), Charles Alston (1907-1977) and Elizabeth Catlett (1915-2012).

3. The *Toussaint L'Ouverture Series* (1938) is in the collection of the Amistad Research Center in New Orleans, Louisiana. The first of Jacob Lawrence's captioned, multi-painting series, it memorialized the life of the important Black resistance leader in verdant colors and moving, figurative flourishes. Nearly fifty years later, Lawrence would create an editioned series of fifteen silkscreens entitled *the Life of Toussaint L'Ouverture* (1986-1997) based on the original 1938 *Toussaint L'Ouverture Series* in tempera. Toussaint L'Ouverture has also been the subject of Haitian-born artist Edouard Duval-Carrie (1954-) in the exhibition *Divine Revolution* at the UCLA Fowler Museum (2004-2005).

A mainstay of Barontini's iconography, the figure of L'Ouverture has appeared in earlier works, including silkscreened and digitally printed fabric capes, chaps, scarves and flags performed and exhibited in *Caribbean Fantasia* at Fort Worth Contemporary Arts in Texas in 2020. The monumental *Caribbean Fantasia Panorama* demonstrates Barontini's clever bricolage of historical and contemporary elements, mixed media and colorful flair pushing back against the constraints of Art History and the conventional techniques of framing and stretching to reveal the vibrant, curved textile work suspended from the ceiling and tethered to the floor. In it, three revolutionary figures appear on horseback wearing military regalia, including the black and white reproduction of an oil painting once believed to be the Black British abolitionist, Olaudah Equiano, a collaged Ife head and a contemporary mashup of L'Ouverture.[4] Barontini's handy splicing and rearranging of these figurative pieces suggest new narratives, while introducing a sense of movement and three-dimensionality. Precursors to the commanding banners and textile works of *We Could Be Heroes, Caribbean Fantasia* set out to define Barontini's arsenal of images, objects and activations: ornamental trimmings consisting of gold rope, fringe, flags and epaulets referencing the pageantry of military service are sewn together with silkscreened images of real and invented revolutionary leaders on horseback or wielding

4. The portrait referenced here once believed to be of Equiano is now titled *Portrait of a Man in a Red Suit*, c. 1757-1760 and it is in the collection of the Royal Albert Memorial Museum in Exeter, Devon, England, accession number 14/1943.

machetes. Elements of abstraction place the figures within a moody landscape, a sky awash in jewel colors, emanating triumph and the fervor of victory. *The Battle of Vertières*, the expansive suspended textile work anchoring the South Transept, employs some of the same strategies pioneered in *Caribbean Fantasia Panorama*, including the clever positioning of archival images and iconographies of Barontini's making as well as the cutting and pasting of historical references, such as military equine statuary, or the powerful imposition of outsized, portraiture. However, in this work as in *The Crossing*, showing opposite in the North Transept, the artist is keen to push back against the tradition of French history painting, notably the series of battle scenes that memorialized the exploits of Napoleon (1769-1821) in the nineteenth century, such as *The Battle of Austerlitz, December 2, 1805* painted by François Gérard (1770-1837) in 1810, which depicts the French defeat of the Russian and Austrian armies led by Napoleon. That monumental canvas dramatizes the moment with General Rapp (1871-1821) presenting Napoleon (at his right surrounded by generals) with the defeated Russian Prince, Nikolai Repnin-Volkonsky (1778-1845). The pageantry of the key figures as well as the supporting roles, with victorious soldiers flanking in the background versus the dead and dying bodies dispersed about the foreground, follows a stated code of battle scene representation that would permeate the genre for the next quarter-century with more than thirty monumental-sized battle scene paintings displayed in the Galerie des Batailles at the Palace of Versailles by 1837.

In contrast, Barontini's *Battle of Vertières* celebrates the pivotal victory of General Jean-Jacques Dessalines (1758-1806), who led the Haitian army after L'Ouverture's death, over France's General Rochambeau (1755-1813) on November 18, 1803, paving the way to the independent nation of Haiti in 1804. With Barontini's now-established iconography, the historical panorama is set in the Caribbean, signaled by the bright color palette as well as the presence of tropical palm trees placed on either side framing the battle scene, the vibrant cannon fire, the figure on horseback

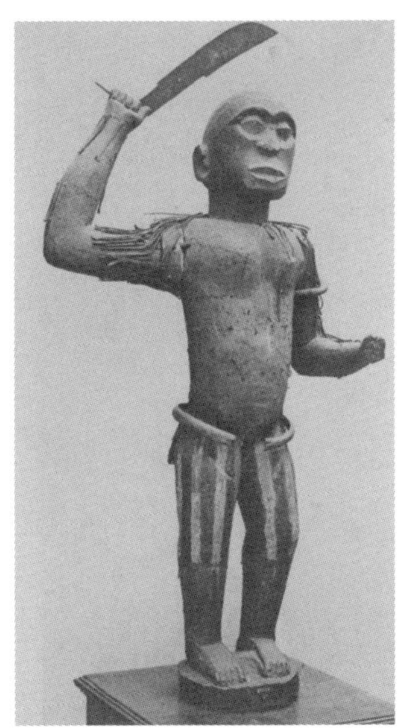

C. Photograph of an anonyme Statue: *Ghézo, roi du Dahomey*, 1943.

5. The Benin ritual figure, formerly in the collection of the musée du quai Branly - Jacques Chirac, was repatriated in 2023 together with a group of twelve other objects following the release of the Sarr Savoy Report commissioned by President Emmanuel Macron and published in 2018.

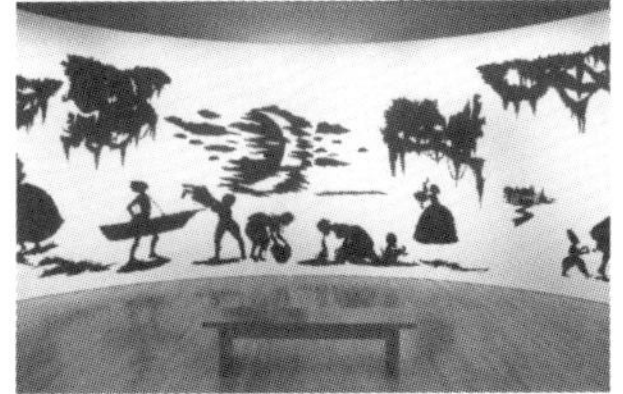

D. Kara Walker, *Slavery! Slavery!*, 1997, cut paper and adhesive on wall, 335 × 2590 cm.

and the ultimate demonstration of victory by the Haitian army. As if narrating the story, an oversized bust of a general at left stares confidently at the viewer, followed by a soldier on horseback with an equally assured look in his eye. At the center, victory is symbolized by an enlarged image of a ritual figure from Benin[C] formerly in the collection of the musée du quai Branly - Jacques Chirac and the bold victory flag above.[5]

The first showing of *The Battle of Vertières* since its debut in *We Could Be Heroes* was at the Currier Museum of Art in New Hampshire in winter-spring 2024. Concurrently on view at the Currier Museum was a presentation of Kara Walker's (1969) critically acclaimed *Harper's Pictorial History of the Civil War (Annotated)*, a portfolio of fifteen prints in which the artist enlarged and reproduced prints from the popular nineteenth-century Civil War account *Harper's Pictorial History of the Civil War* (Chicago, 1862), and overlaid silkscreened silhouette figures in solid black[D], reminiscent of her well-known practice. In her seminal work from the 1990s, Walker took the late seventeenth and early eighteenth-century representational silhouette portrait miniature and enlarged it to life-size, creating panoramic murals of cut-out, black figures set against stark, white walls. By enlarging the silhouette figures to life-size and introducing a narrative function, Walker revolutionized the 200-year-old portrait medium and innovated the nascent 1990s-era practice of installation with life-sized panoramic murals. Viewers could relate to these works at a bodily scale through their 1:1 relationship to the figures in the murals, further enriching the storytelling capabilities of these works. Similarly, Barontini's banners and panoramas have a kinesthetic relationship to the viewer at the level of scale, enhanced by their accessible tactile qualities as well as their subversive narrative function. The translation between scale offers a new way of seeing and experiencing these works, where you can relate your human self to them and become part of the narrative. Barontini's practice of cutting up a painting, print, photograph or sculpture and re-piecing it together, retelling the story with the figures he inserts, activates them with vitality and movement while offering alternative narratives inclusive of Caribbean histories. Updating and rewriting histories is something that both Barontini and Walker do well with their use of novel techniques and historical archives.

Photography and the Art of Mechanical Reproduction

Photography plays an important role in the work of Raphaël Barontini as it does in the history of art, the evolution of Enlightenment-era vision, the documentation of the colonial project and the accumulation of archives. While formally introduced to the world commercially in 1839 by Louis Jacques Mandé Daguerre (1787-1851) in France and William Henry Fox Talbot (1800-1877) in England, the photograph was a product of the Enlightenment and the technology pioneered to make it resulted in new ways of seeing that affected not only human interaction but also the history of art, notions of truth and the ability to document the colonial era with images of conquest of foreign lands and peoples as well as images of cultural artifacts, architecture, flora and fauna.[6] The resulting collections of objects and their documentation, and archives to hold them, have become the rich fodder of Barontini's innovative practice, making these seemingly historical images feel presciently contemporary through cutting, splicing, and suturing as well as with proportion, placement, repetition and alignment. This practice has an impact on the viewer, of course, but it also purposely brings to the fore the violence of slavery and colonialism through the cut and reattachment, the movement and realignment, the free license with scale, saturation, coloration and repetition. With access to the archives of the Louvre, the Bibliothèque nationale de France, the Amistad Research Center and more, Barontini has conjured his own visual language out of amended historical and archival images as a form of repair.

6. Prior to 1839, Joseph Nicéphore Niépce, a French inventor, had pioneered the heliograph, the closest precursor to photography as we know it. Taking over for history painting by the late 1840s, photography photographers regularly accompanied colonial expeditions and were present on the battlefield.

Collage-Bricolage

Collage and bricolage disrupt the linearity of historical narratives and open new spaces, playing fields of understanding for unheard voices, stories of the underrepresented and ignored to be seen, heard, rewritten, and told anew. Harnessing and imbuing images of the past with future possibility, Barontini creates novel forms of storytelling where portraiture, iconography, performance and the Black body land in the gaps, suture, heal and release, challenging how, who and what we remember in the most coveted and defining of national memorials in France, the Panthéon. Amplifying and updating the power of bricolage, the textile works, banners, sonic landscape and performance of *We Could Be Heroes* are put in service to honor the unacknowledged freedom fighters, maroons, and revolutionary leaders of the Caribbean (Guadeloupe, Martinique, and Haiti), who fought vigorously for freedom and self-determination, eschewing centuries-old master narratives to acknowledge and propose new possibilities. Culling, splicing and reinserting images from the archives and collections of French national museums, Barontini transforms the celebrated form of the eighteenth and nineteenth-century history painting for a twenty-first-century audience, creating massive, panoramic historical textile works that span the North and South Transepts of the Panthéon, positioned to capture the changing light of the fall and winter skies, adding layers to the atmospheric mood of the overall work. Inspired, in part, by his training at the École nationale supérieure des beaux-arts de Paris and his studio across the street from the Louvre, Barontini rightfully has questioned the historical narratives of France's most illustrious museum and the stories that have been forgotten, elided, untold. A shrewd observer of history and art, Barontini has studied the paintings at the Louvre, the Palace of Versailles and other national and global museums, deciphering their iconographies and codes, taking account of the missing narratives. In addition to history painting, the ritual objects stolen from African societies during colonization also form part of his visual language.

Residencies and Commissions

Since the Renaissance, with the establishment of the Accademia delle Arti del Disegno in Florence, Italy, artist residencies have played a pivotal role in the history of art and inspired artistic innovation.[7] In addition to providing studio space and access to skills-building and training, they have long been an important

7. In 1563, the Duke of Florence, Cosimo de' Medici, and Tuscan painter Giorgio Vasari co-established the Accademia delle Arti del Disegno in Florence, Italy. Serving as a pioneering art institution, the Accademia was the first to advocate for the notion that artists could derive benefits from a dedicated local space aimed at advancing their skills.

part of artist development and education, fostering exposure to new materials, techniques and cultures, while expanding networks between artists and patrons alike. For Barontini, artist residencies have enabled him to experiment, learn and grow for more than a decade. In 2013, he was selected for the Périféériques (Chantiers du Sud) residency in Jacmel, Haiti, where he lived in a Vodou temple for one month and received lessons every morning, learning Vodou ceremonial rituals that later influenced his own use of performance as a transformational element of his multidisciplinary artistic practice. According to the artist, the residency in Haiti "helped me to understand the history of the Caribbean," while emphasizing the distinct histories of Francophone Caribbean and Indian Ocean islands—the people, landscapes and resources—and how they were emboldened by the resistance to slavery and colonization through self-emancipatory practices such as marronage and creolized religions like Vodou.[8]

8. Raphaël Barontini interview with Cheryl Finley, July 5, 2024.

Like artist residencies, public commissions also have a way of challenging artists' methodologies and reshaping their practices. As site-specific engagements, public commissions call upon artists to consider locale, including history, community and materials. In 2019, Barontini was awarded a public commission by the Savannah College of Art and Design (SCAD) in Georgia that resulted in his first solo exhibition and performance in the US, *the Golden March*, which explored the life of legendary abolitionist and activist Frederick Douglass. This commission proved decisive in the artist's career with its bold application of the archives and performance to challenge and subvert traditional modes of representation. It reaffirmed his novel use of layered silkscreens sourced from historic paintings, prints and photographs found in the archives of Black resistance to slavery to tell the story of Douglass' escape from slavery to freedom in the North in 1838. Printed on hand-dyed textiles, with the addition of ceremonial elements, including fringe, banners and satin, these works were activated in a parade orchestrated by Barontini when he enlisted the talents of a local high school marching band. His commission at SCAD, together with his earlier residency in Haiti, revealed connections between the American South and the islands of the Francophone Caribbean through the narratives of indigenous and African-descended peoples' resistance to slavery and colonialism. Together, these distinct yet interconnected diasporic histories, cultures and practices prepared Barontini for the Panthéon commission.

Textiles and Collaborating with the Next Generation

Textiles are foundational to Barontini's practice, and their versatility has equipped him with innovative ways to think beyond traditional canvas stretchers, off the wall, as well as through installation and performance. The materiality of the fabric banners enabled visitors to be more in touch with the artwork. According to the artist, "What I wanted with my fabric and textile installation was for people to be involved in the topic and subject of the installation due to the size and materiality."[9]

9. Raphaël Barontini in conversation with Cheryl Finley, March 29, 2024.

The photographic nature of the imagery and iconography also lends a certain familiarity to contemporary audiences while the banners, positioned at the entrance to the Panthéon, take a stand, subvert what is around them and confront the viewer upon entry.

Partnering with local Carnival bands wherever he exhibits lends greater access to Barontini's work, conveying his messages and teachings more freely through the visitor's relationship to performance and the kinesthetic experience of installation. Consciously working with communities in Saint-Denis or in communities nearby where he is exhibiting, Barontini has worked closely with local art schools, textile students, dancers and Caribbean Carnival troupes. His interest in the practices of Carnival and subversion gave sharper focus to his practice of splicing historic prints, photographs of African ancestral figures and equestrian figures, of layering, transposing and piecing these together, bringing eighteenth and nineteenth-century images into focus for present-day audiences.

Noting the ceremonial purpose of the Panthéon, Barontini treated the commission as an opportunity to pay homage to the hitherto unacknowledged African-descended freedom fighters, leaders and supporters who conspired to defeat slavery and colonialism in the overseas territories. Lining the entrance to the Panthéon, he strategically placed a phalanx of ten textile banners in formation,

five on each side, with life-sized collaged portraits of revolutionary leaders on canvas. The banners are screenprinted on canvas all in the same dimension, with great attention to detailed handwork. One cannot visually see a collage with different materials like the large panoramic pieces in the North and South transepts, which are pieced-together collages. Instead, the banners are pictorial works with a flat appearance, which Barontini intended to be activated in the performance. When the banners were completed, he cut, shaped and added the fringe and ceremonial elements to the front and dyed the cotton lining, which he applied to the other side.
The banners' illusory portrait images[E] are sourced from the archives of the musée du quai Branly - Jacques Chirac, the Bibliothèque nationale de France and the repositories of national museums, including classical statuary from the Louvre, to create figures with monumental sensibilities, aligning with the monumentality of the Panthéon itself. Cut, layered and combined with reference images from national memorials, including the symbolic, victorious equestrian statues often associated with military pursuits, Napoleon or his generals (who are buried in the crypt and which Barontini reclaims for his own incisive use) or emboldened examples of classical African sculpture, these imaginary portraits represent ten distinct historical figures, based on the biographical attributes of each character and their corresponding landscapes, creating a cartography of figures from the different Francophone Caribbean and Indian Ocean islands. For example, Reunion Island is represented by a couple. Solitude and Toussaint L'Ouverture are figured in the large-scale textiles in the South Transept. In the end, Barontini's pictorial banners honor figures of resistance and push back against canonical ways to represent them. As key elements of the ceremonial performance directed by Barontini, the pictorial banners were activated by the Mas Choukaj collective, wielding the percussive historical might of Guadeloupean mas Carnival in honoring the dead. Time-based, interactive components of gesture and choreography demonstrated the power of memory secreted in the bodies of the performers, awakening the dead, liberating the spirits of revolution. Ushering the potential of their long-awaited dreams, wishes and desires, on cue from Barontini,

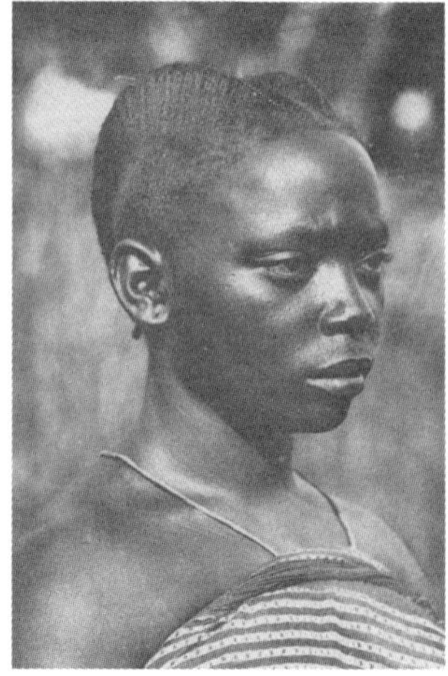
E. Postcard "Makele woman (Aruwimi)".

they march through the gates of the Panthéon to release them anew. Barontini worked closely with students of the École supérieure des arts appliqués Duperré in Paris to create the costumes worn by the Mas Choukaj collective, Caribbean Carnival musicians based in Seine-Saint-Denis, who marked the opening and closing of *We Could Be Heroes* with unforgettable, percussive performances worthy of awakening the dead. The banners and flags installed as a ceremonial arrangement just beyond the entrance to the monument form the artist's own Panthéon of historical and imaginary figures in the fight to end slavery. These include men and women known to have shaped the outcome of the Haitian Revolution, such as Sanite Bélair, Dutty Boukman, Jean-Baptiste Belley and Cécile Fatiman as well as prominent revolutionaries in Guadeloupe and Martinique as well as other overseas territories and maroons, who helped lead the way to freedom. Their figurative representations appear on flags and banners as composite and often imagined images, where no record was found, using pictures from prints, photographs and sculpture, while ornate gold rope, reflective fabrics and dye-transfer create complex images representative of key historical figures. Mounted on poles, these banners and flags were danced as part of the Carnival procession that ultimately led the spirits out an open door in the direction of the setting sun. Raphaël Barontini's Panthéon commission was a monumental undertaking, indeed, charged with addressing the centuries-long absence of national heroes of African and Afro-Caribbean descent in the Panthéon. In the hands of Barontini, how is French national history and memory being challenged anew? By telling a story from the perspective of the indigenous and formerly enslaved, previously overlooked in historical narratives of the victors and figures buried in the Panthéon, Barontini's historic intervention leads the way to consider new methods of memorializing overlooked and unacknowledged historical figures, including everyday women and men, while also proposing actions to provide remedy and inspiration for communities in the present. With this new canon of historical figures offered and envisioned by Barontini, artists, intellectuals, activists, statespeople and students can participate in a national healing of enduring promise. ◆

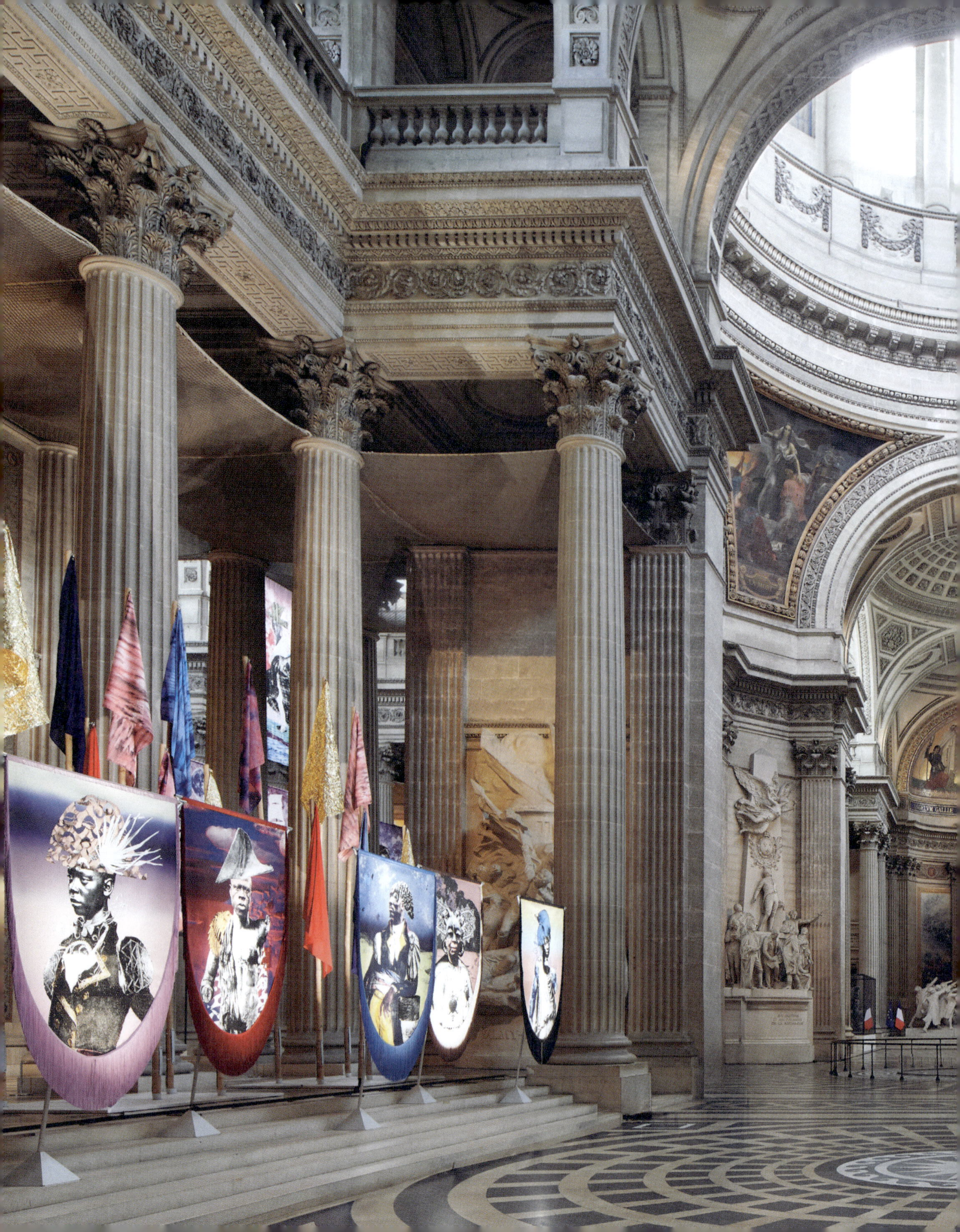

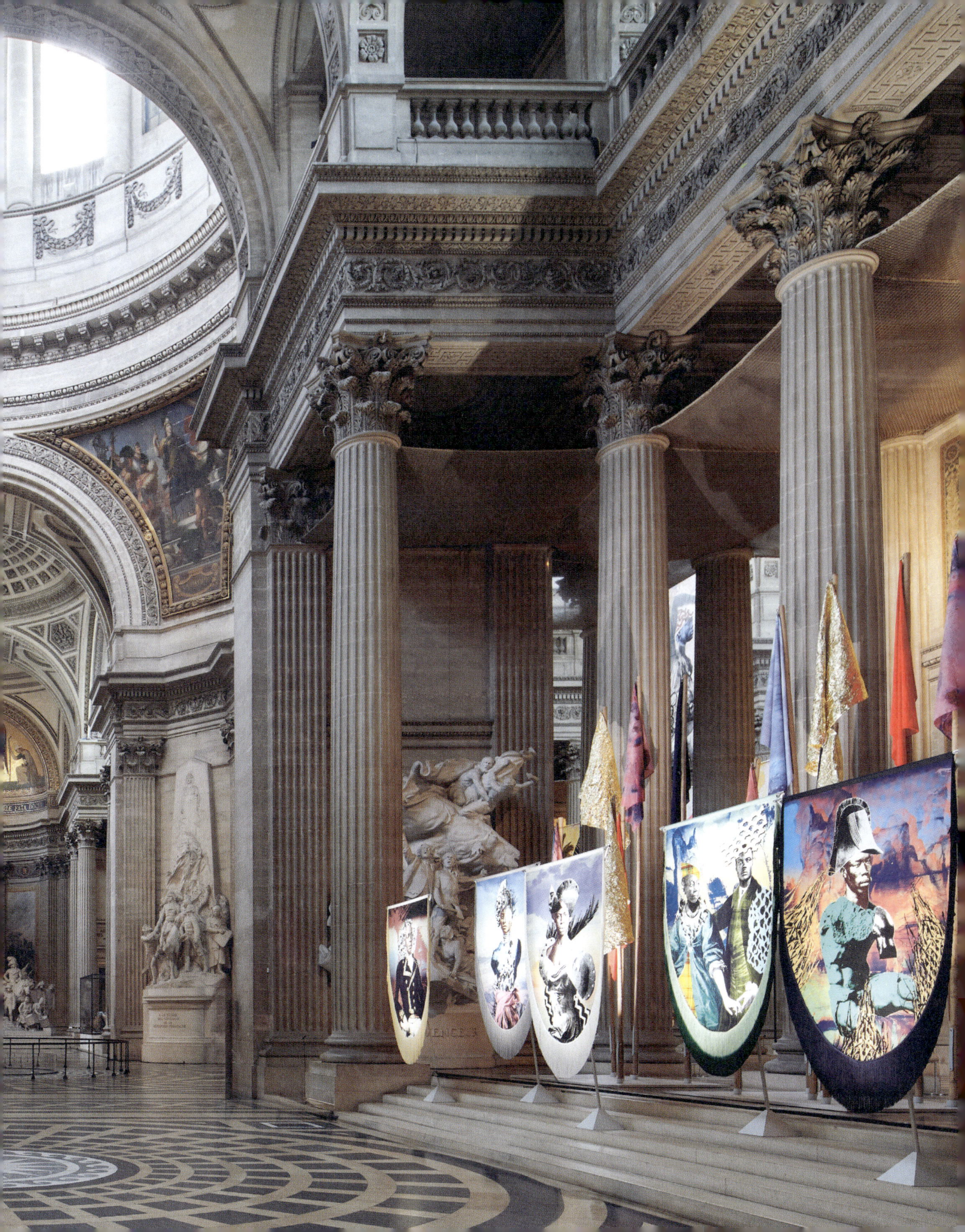

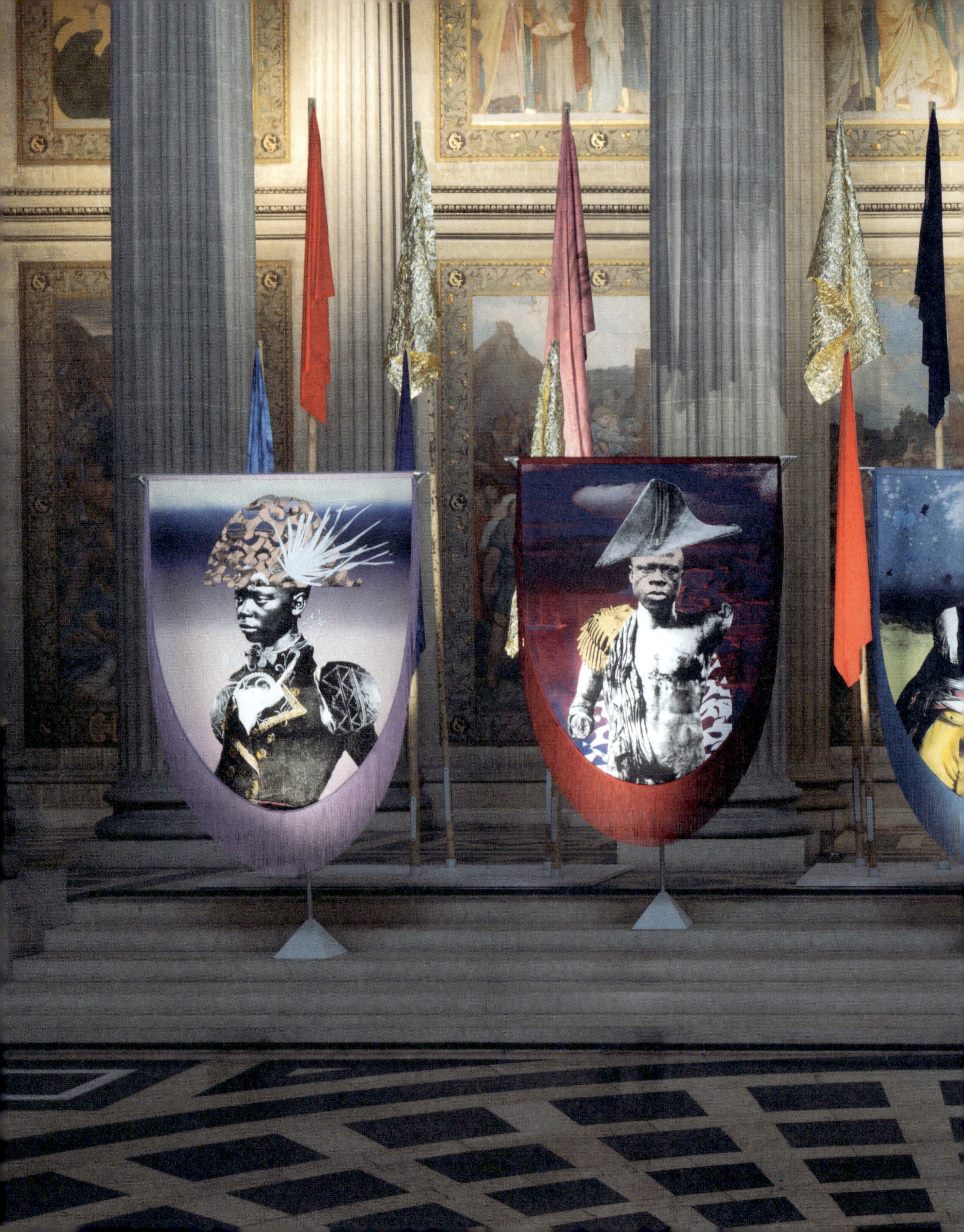

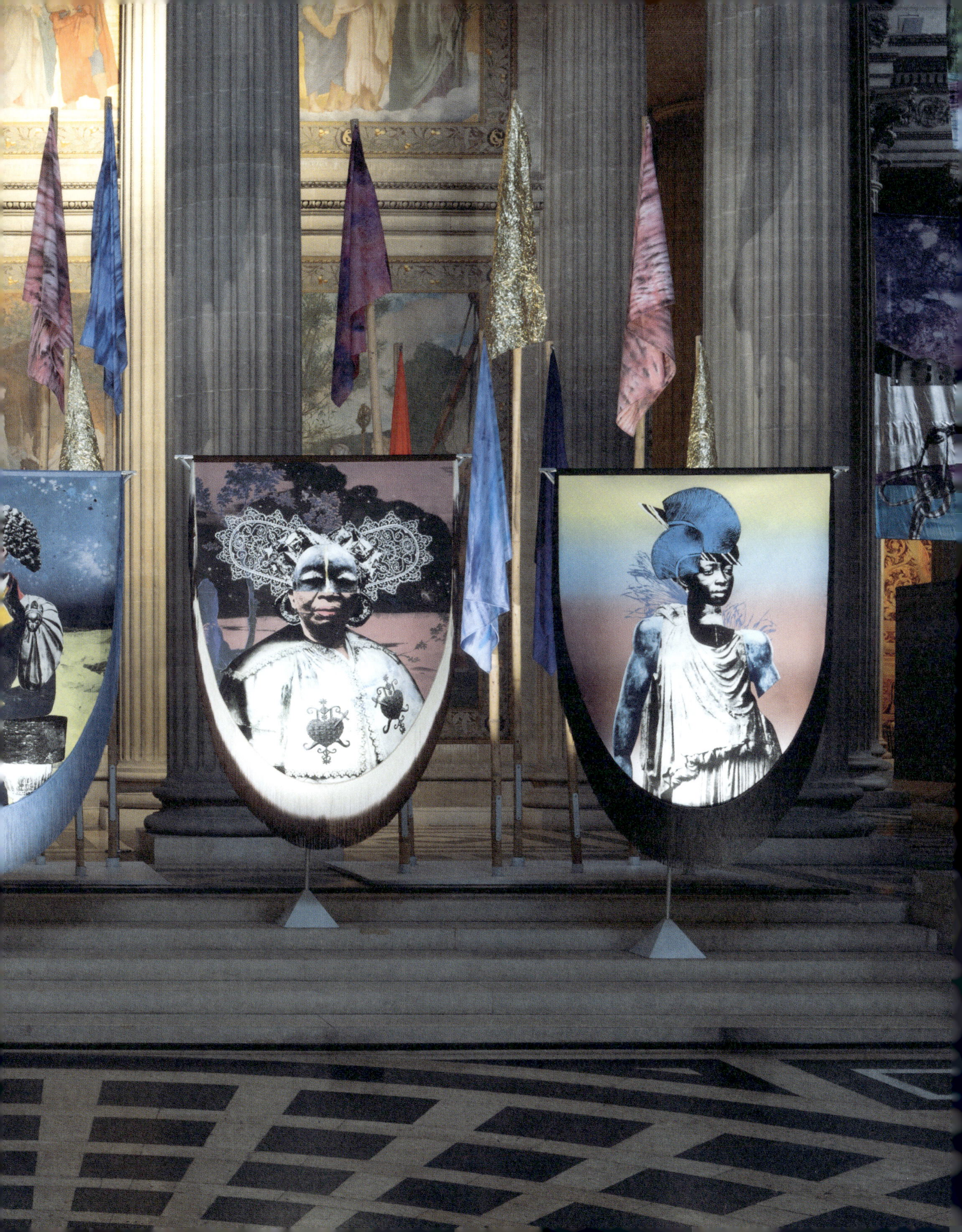

p. 33 *Sanité Belair*, 2023
p. 34 *Voodoo March – Dutty Boukman*, 2023
p. 35 *Voodoo March – Dutty Boukman* (detail), 2023
p. 36 *The Black Jacobin* (detail), 2023
p. 37 *The Black Jacobin*, 2023
p. 38-39 *The Mambo of Bois-Caïman – Cécile Fatiman* (detail), 2023

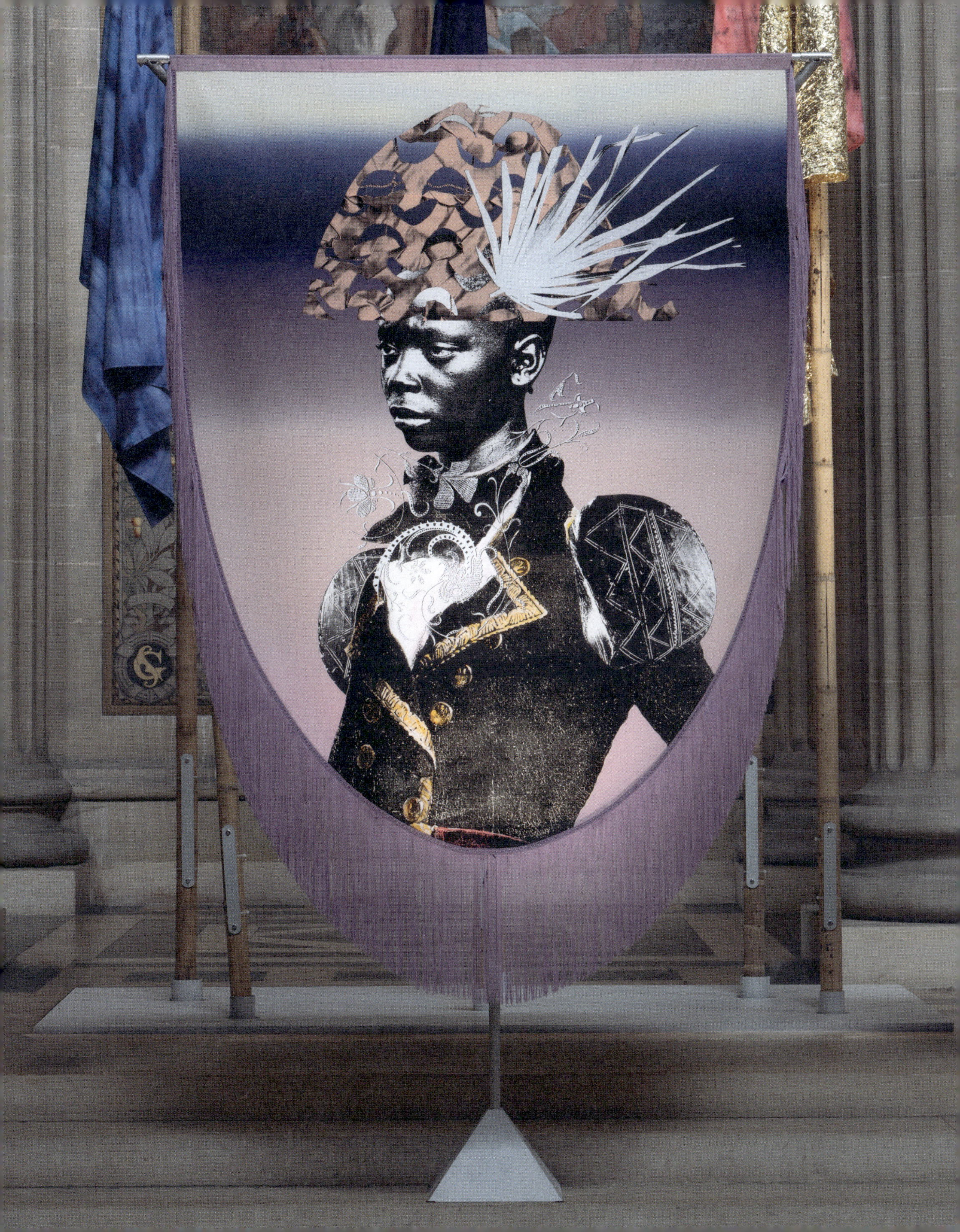

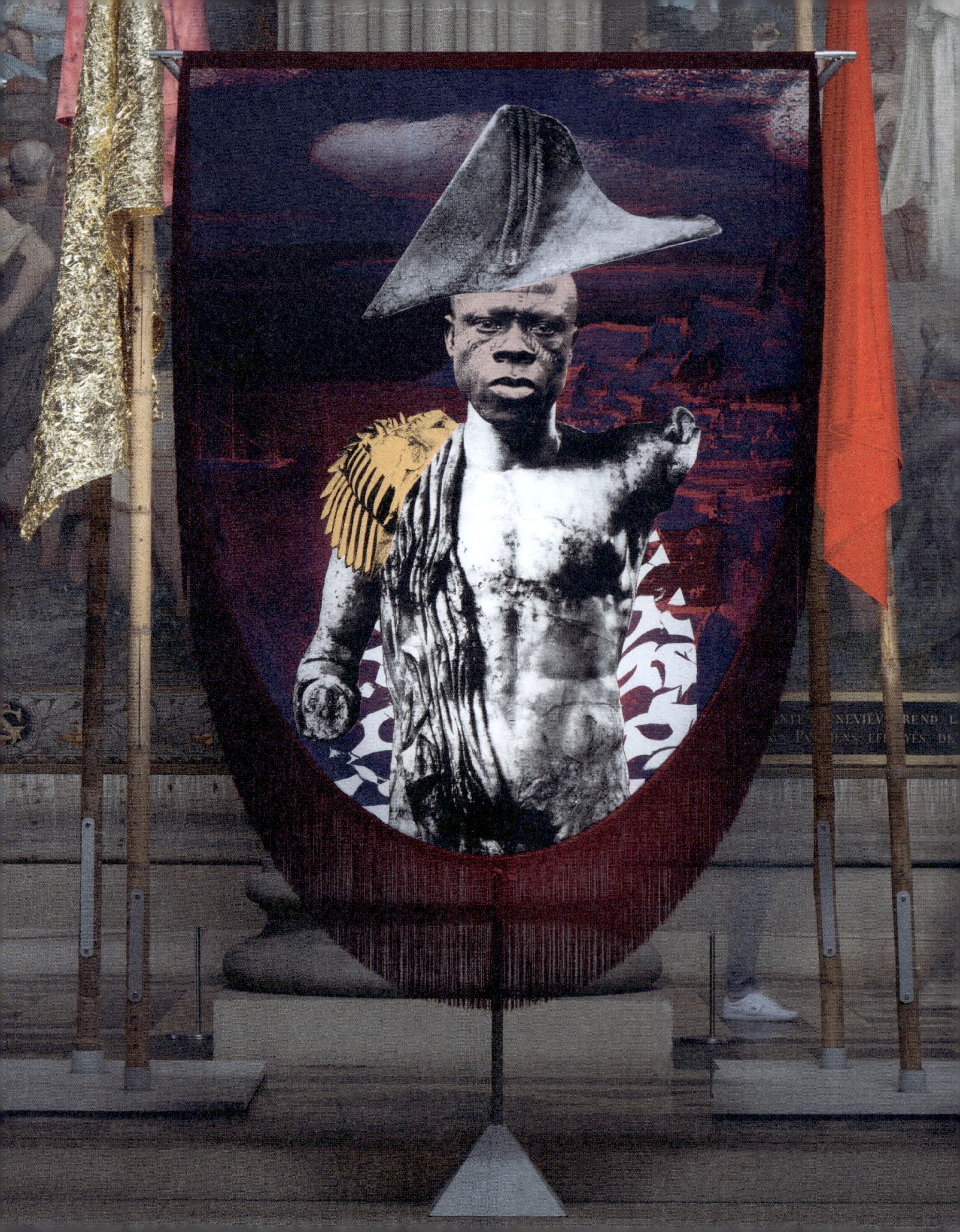

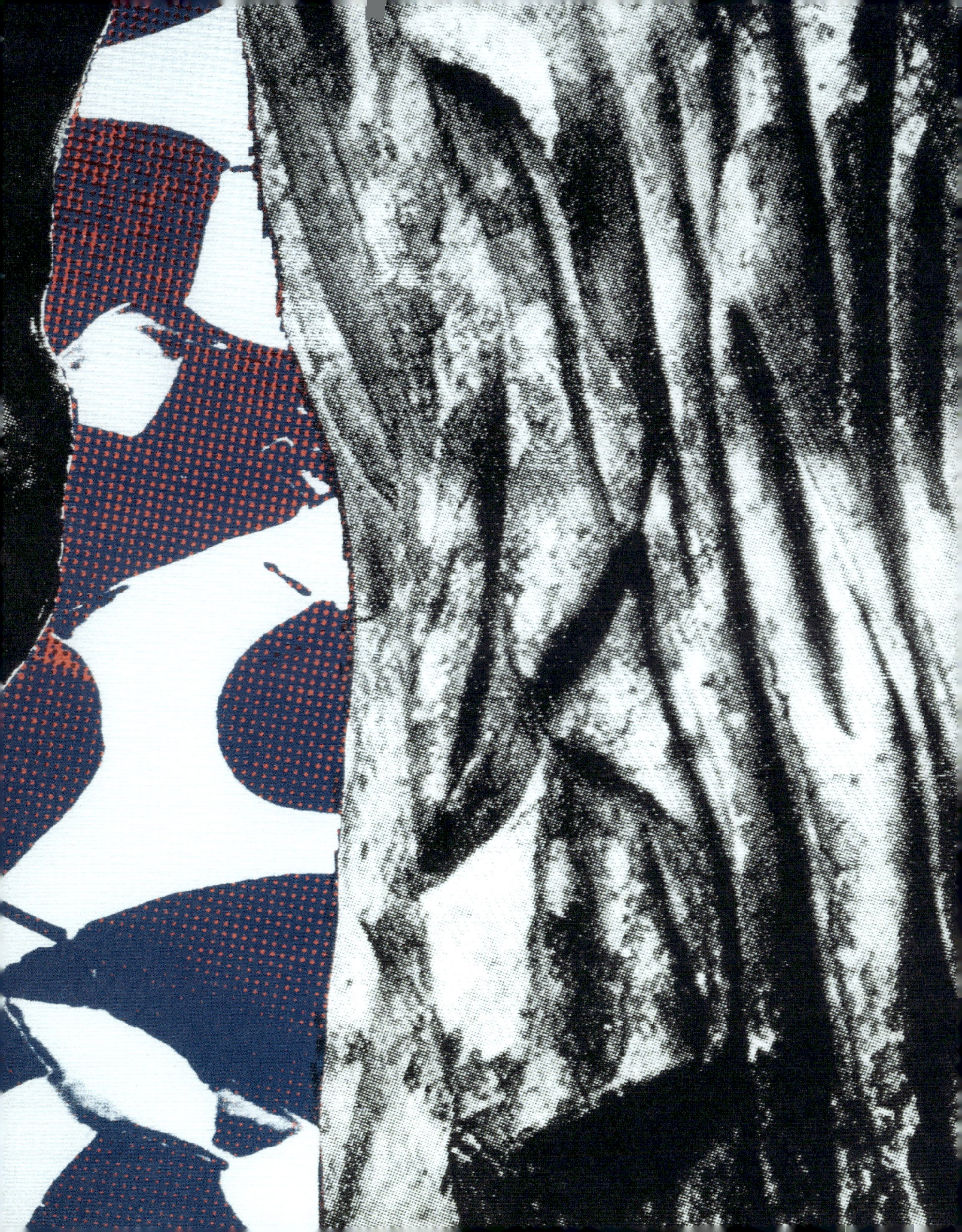

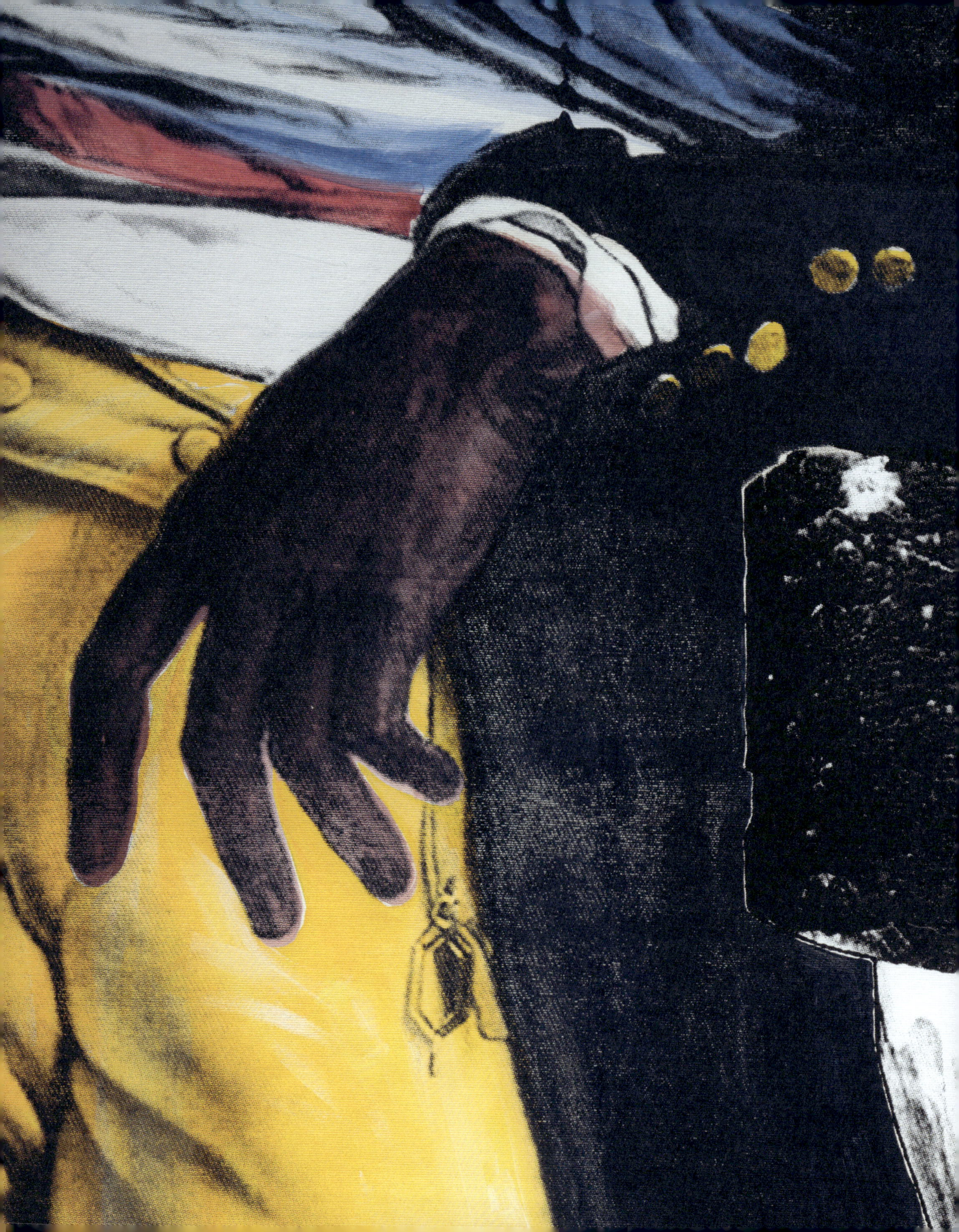

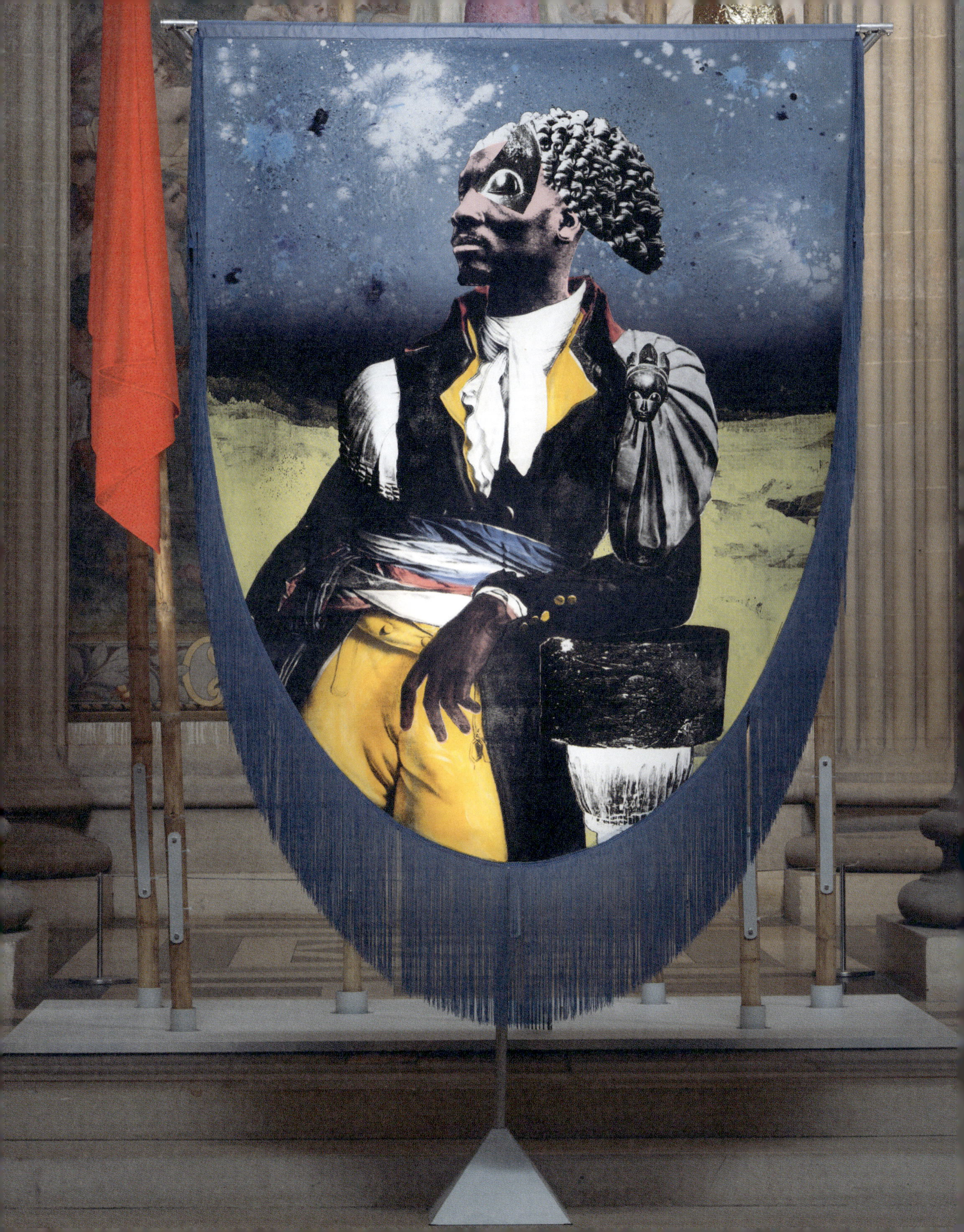

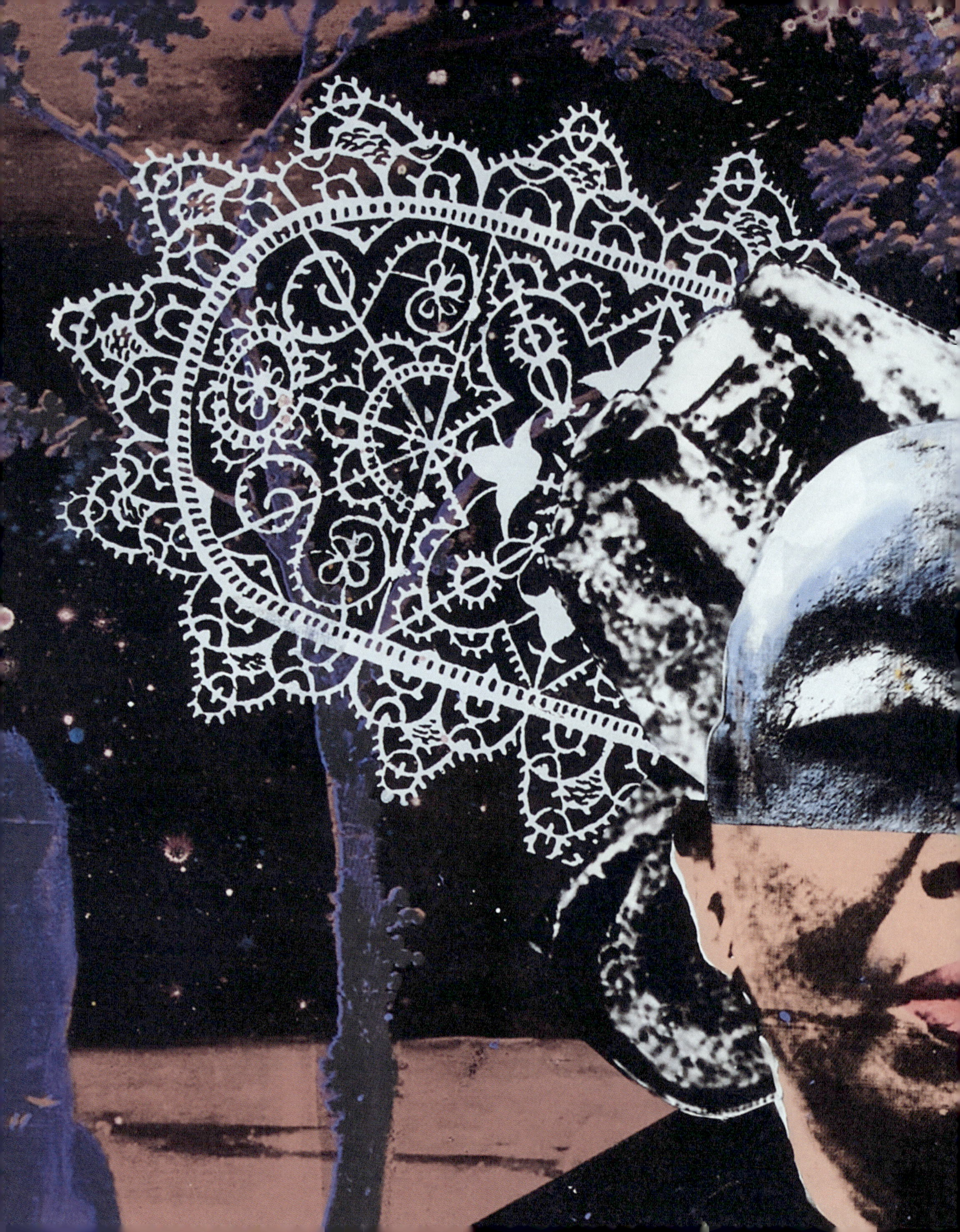

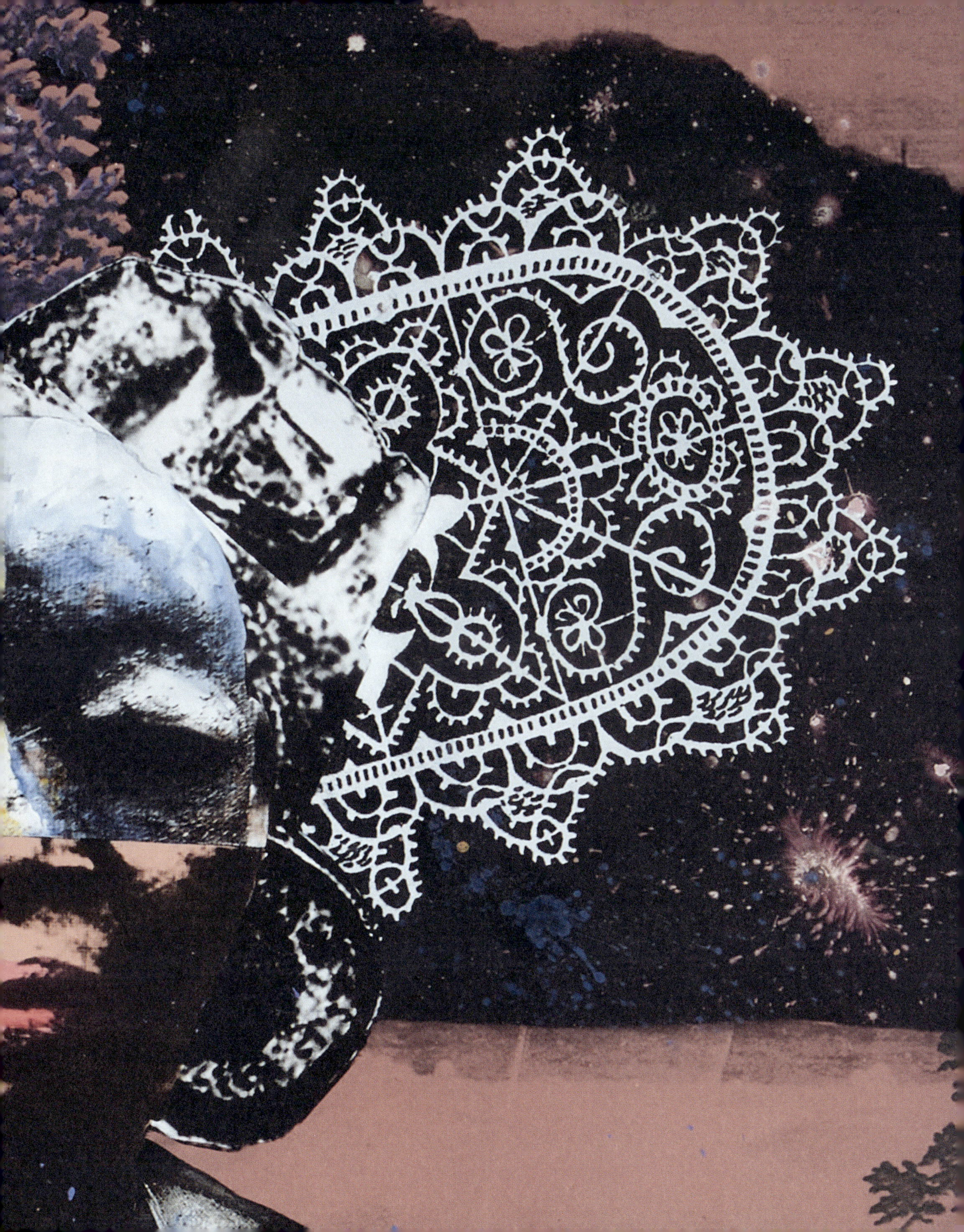

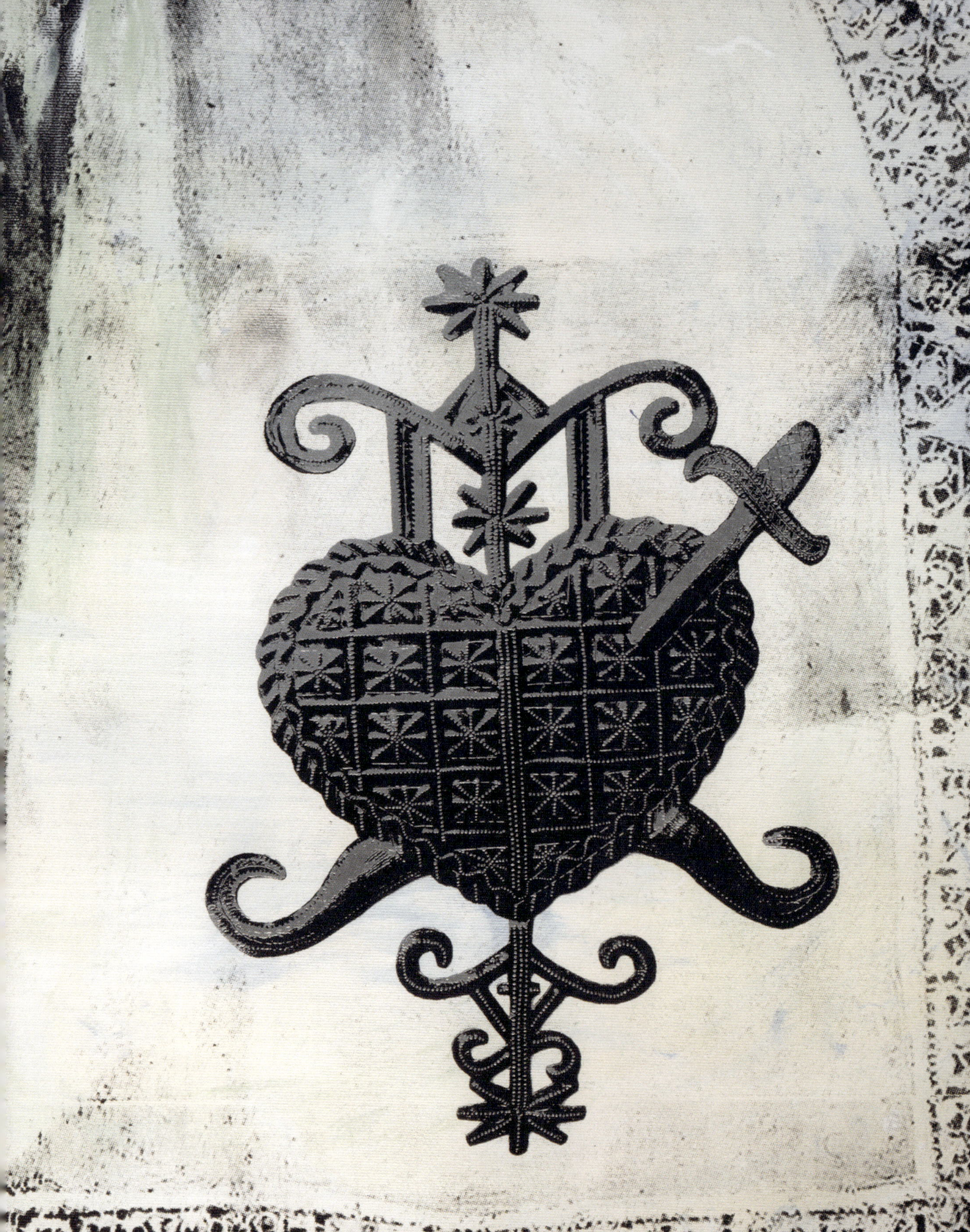

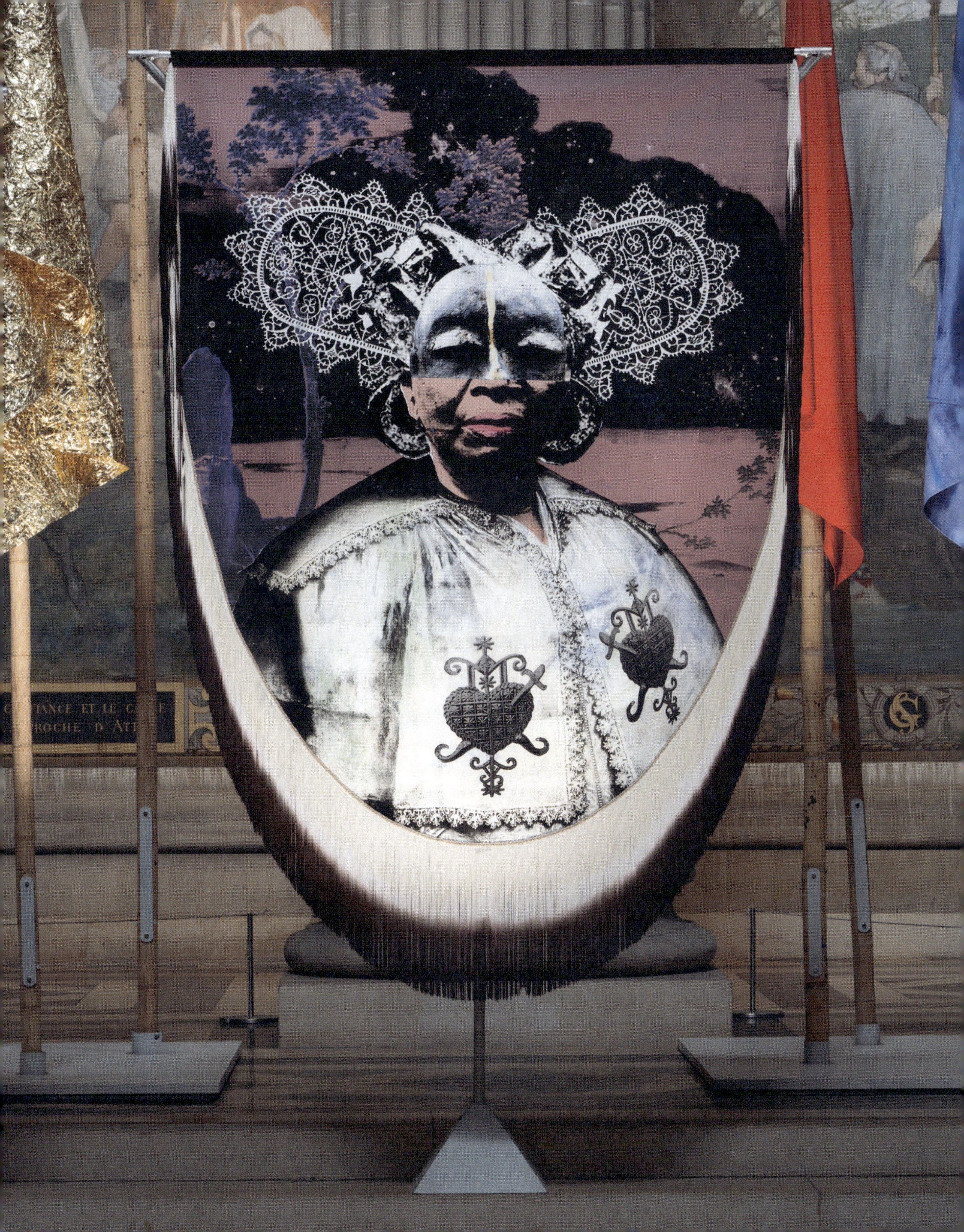

p. 40 *The Mambo of Bois-Caïman – Cécile Fatiman* (detail), 2023
p. 41 *The Mambo of Bois-Caïman – Cécile Fatiman*, 2023
p. 43 *Ormerod*, 2023

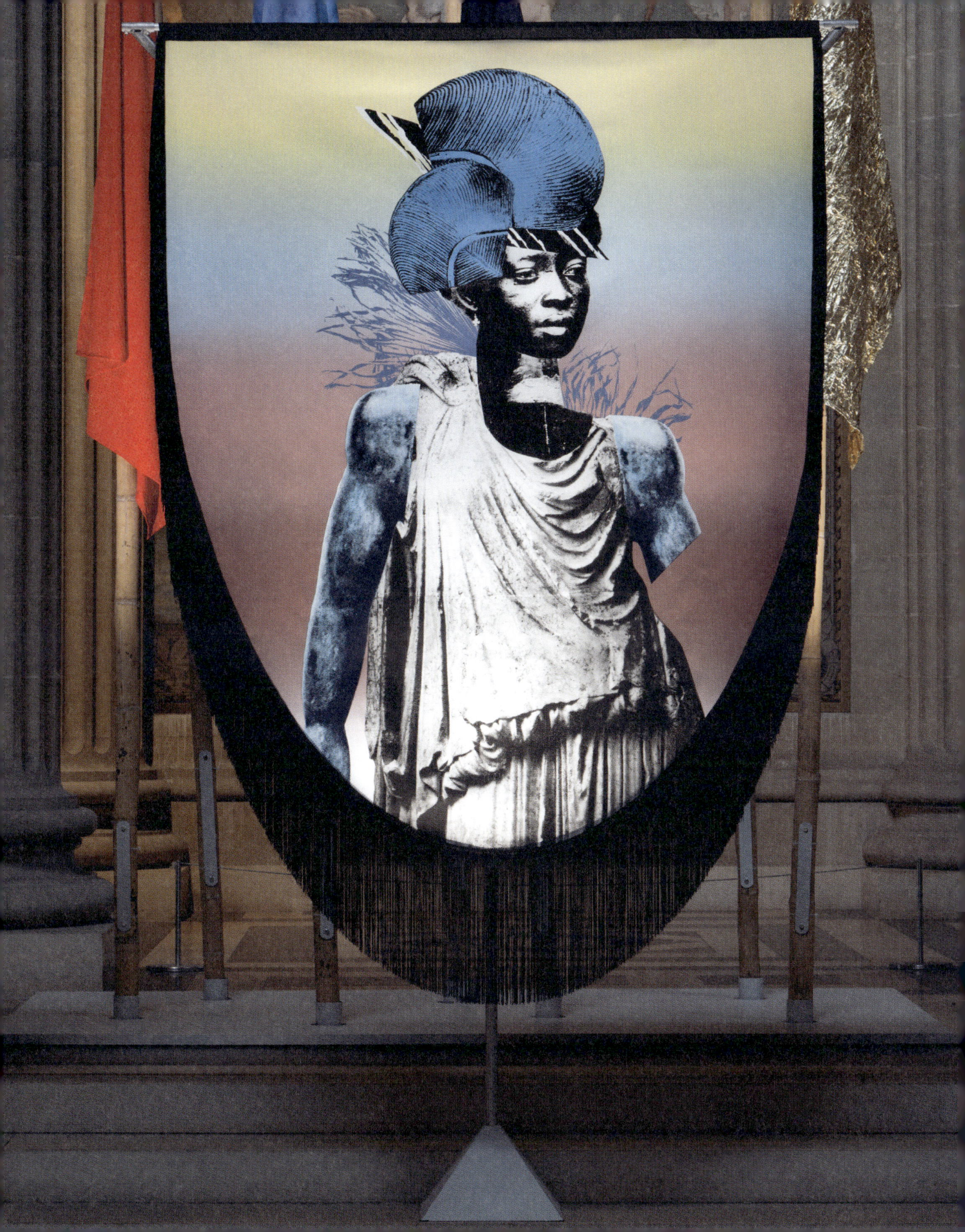

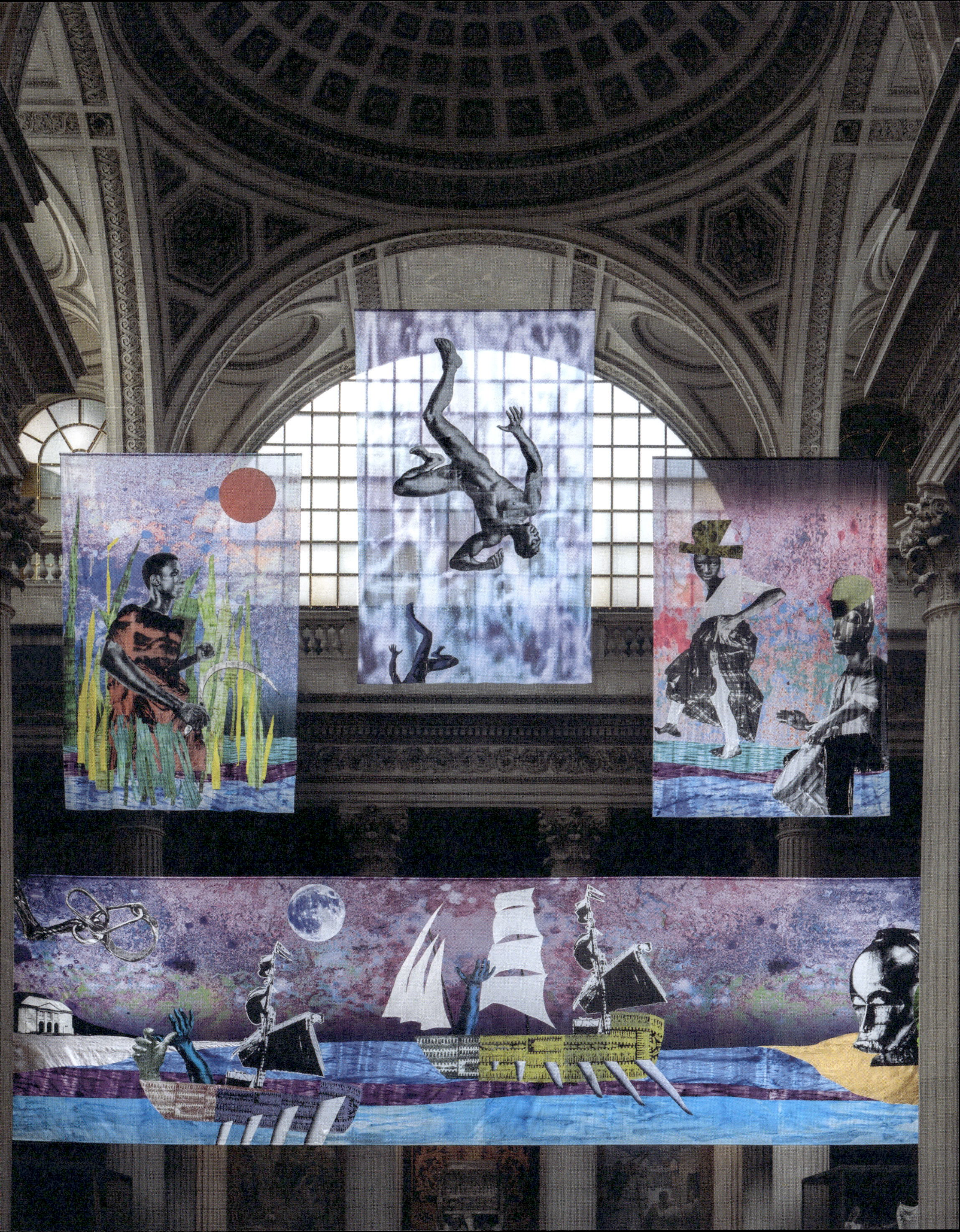

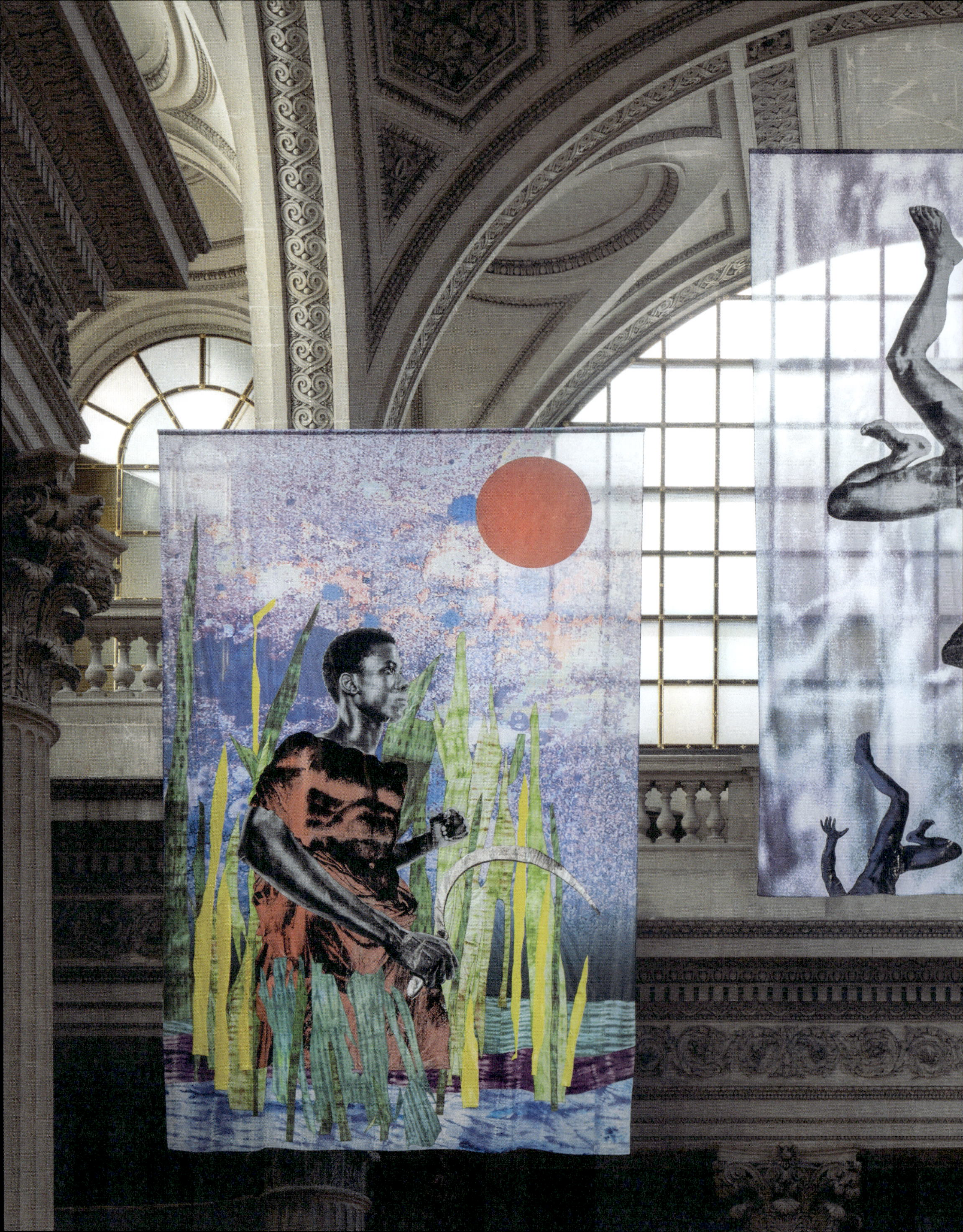

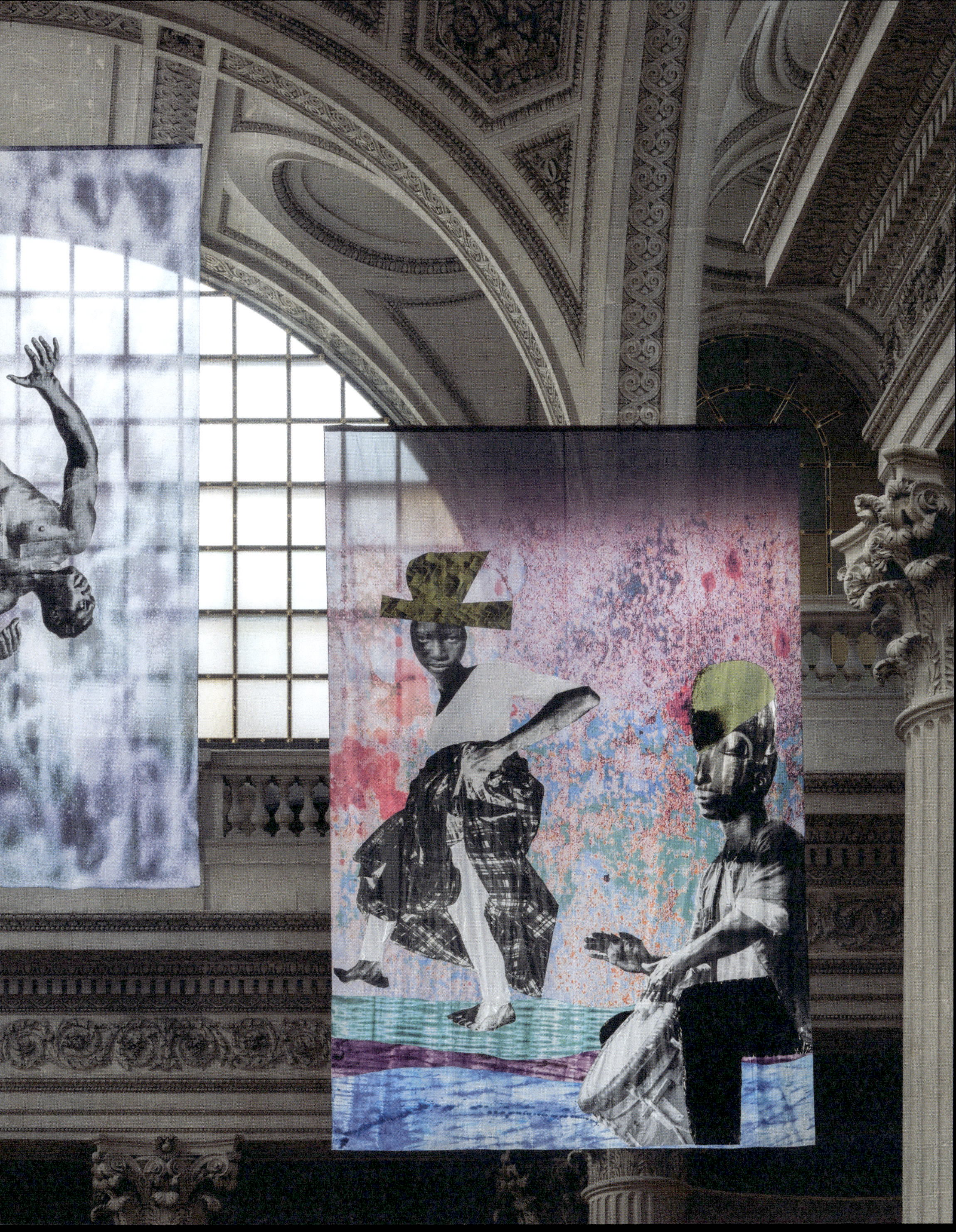

p. 49 *Léwoz* (detail), 2023

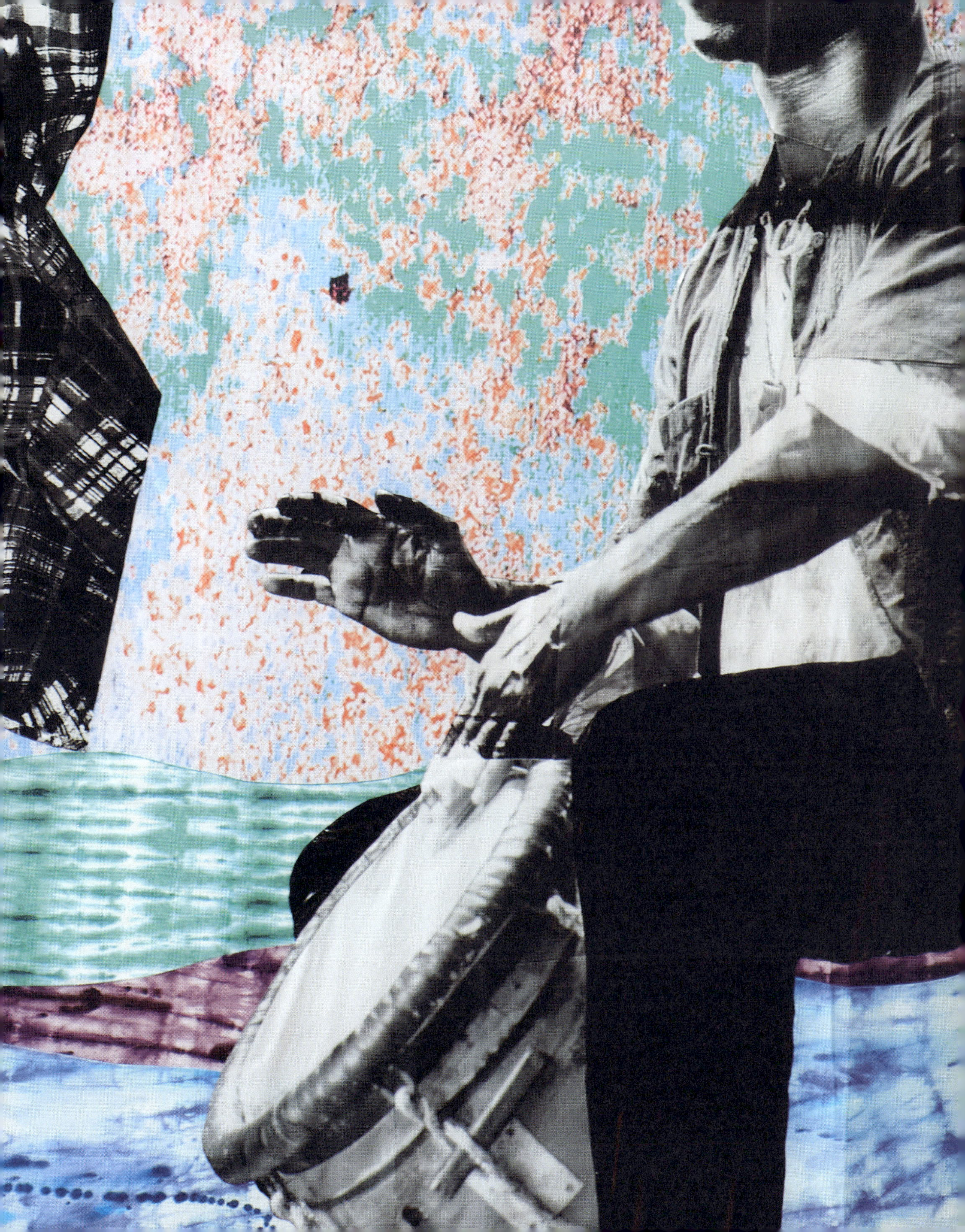

p. 51 *The Maroon*, 2023
p. 52-53 *The Crossing* (detail), 2023

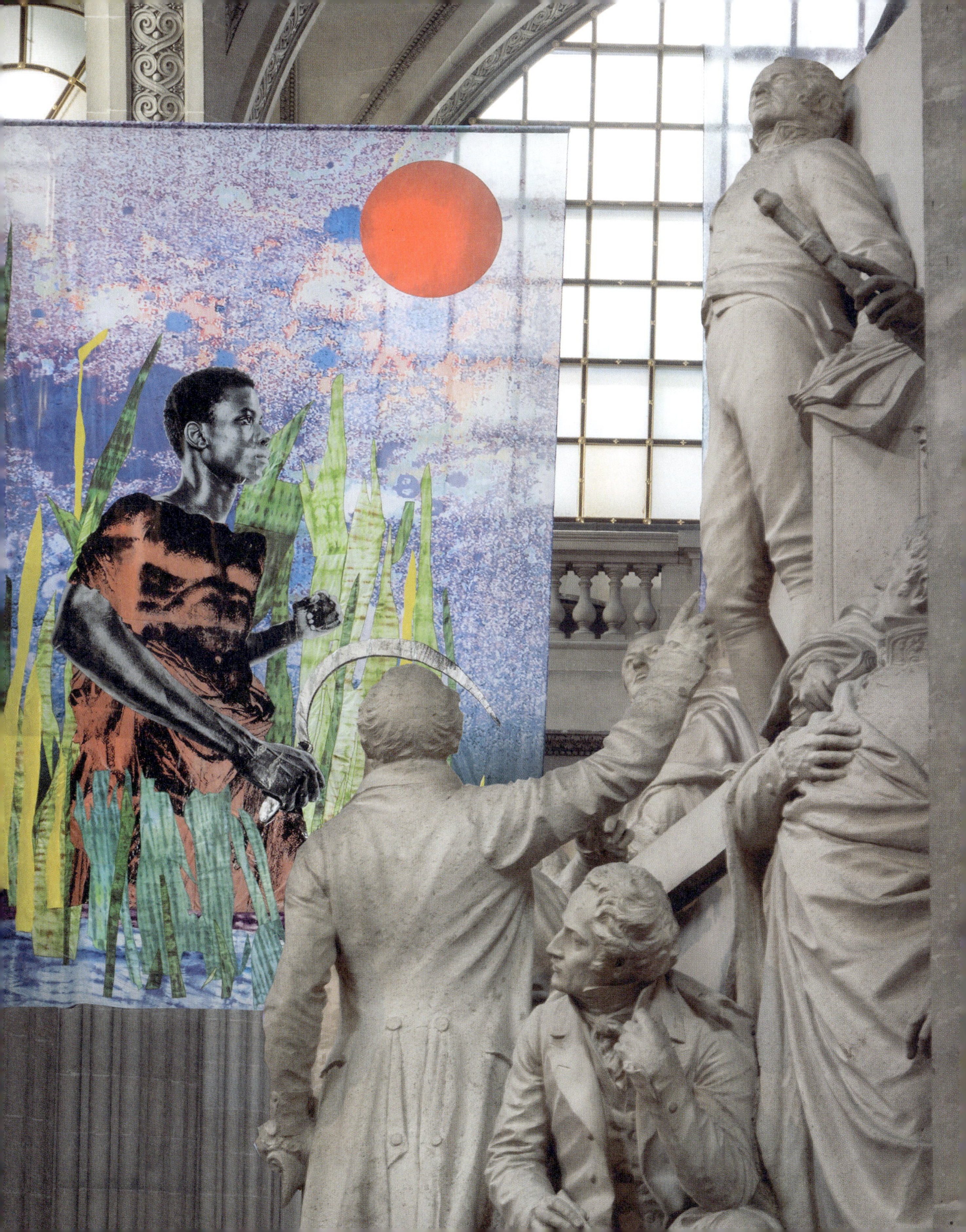

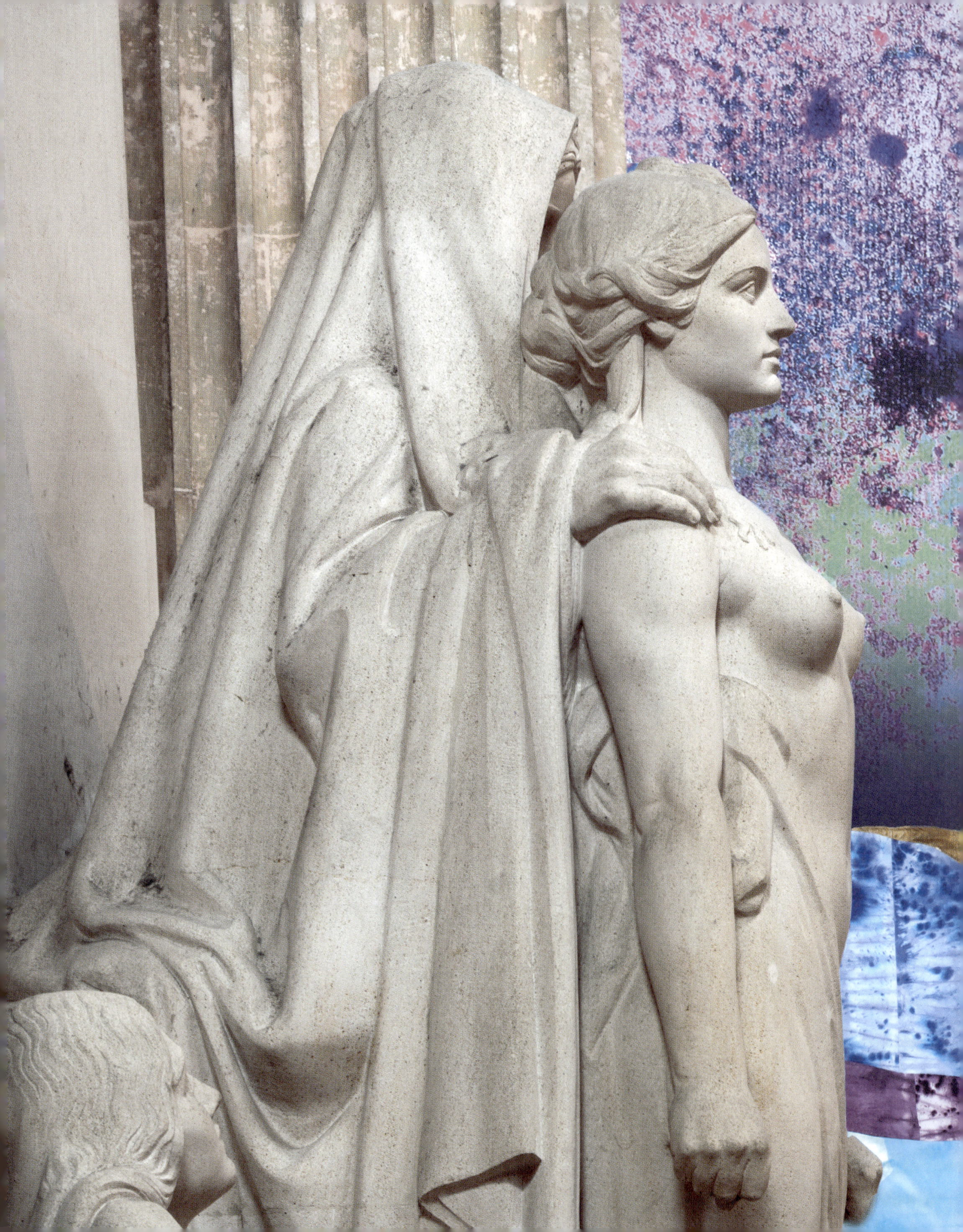

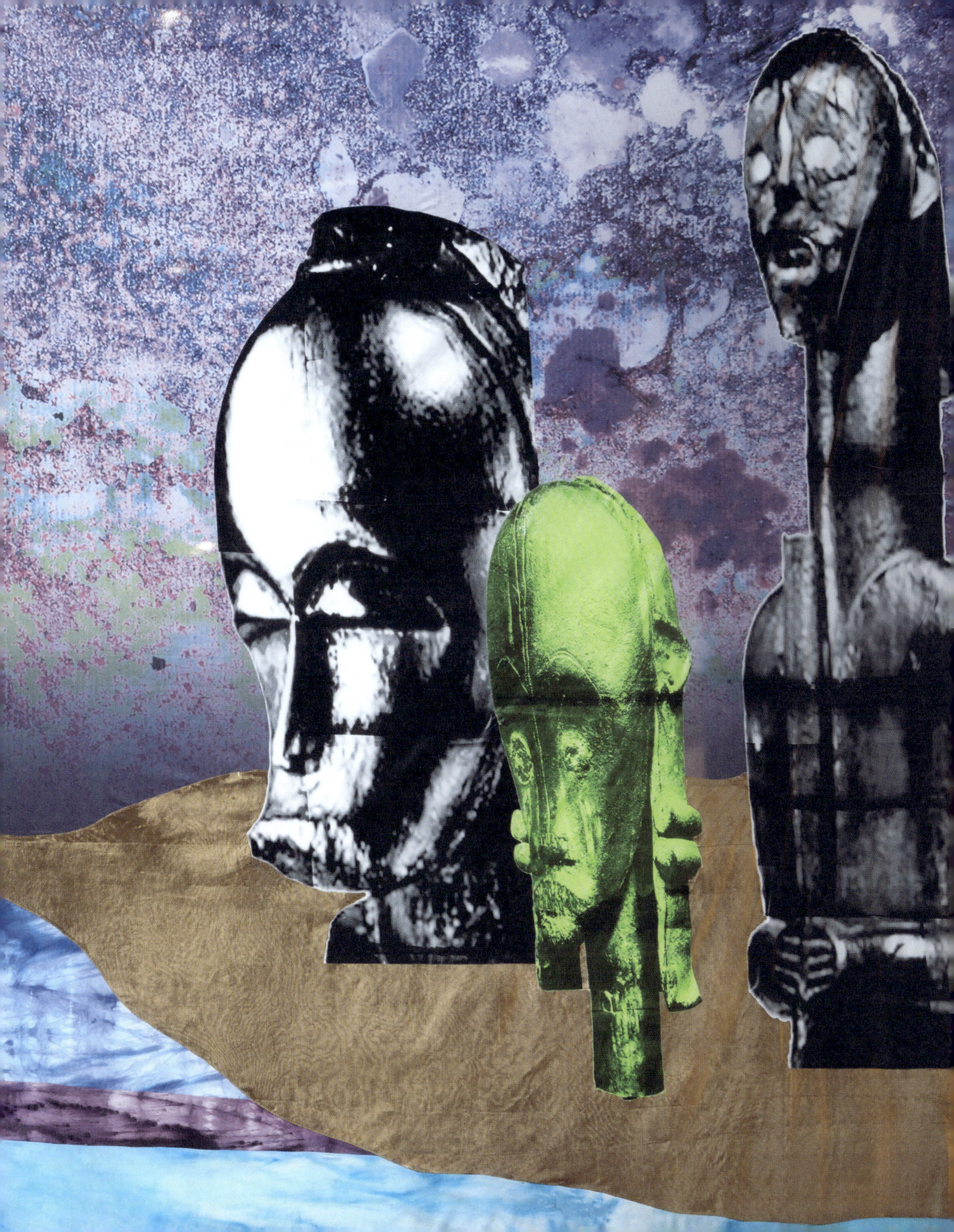

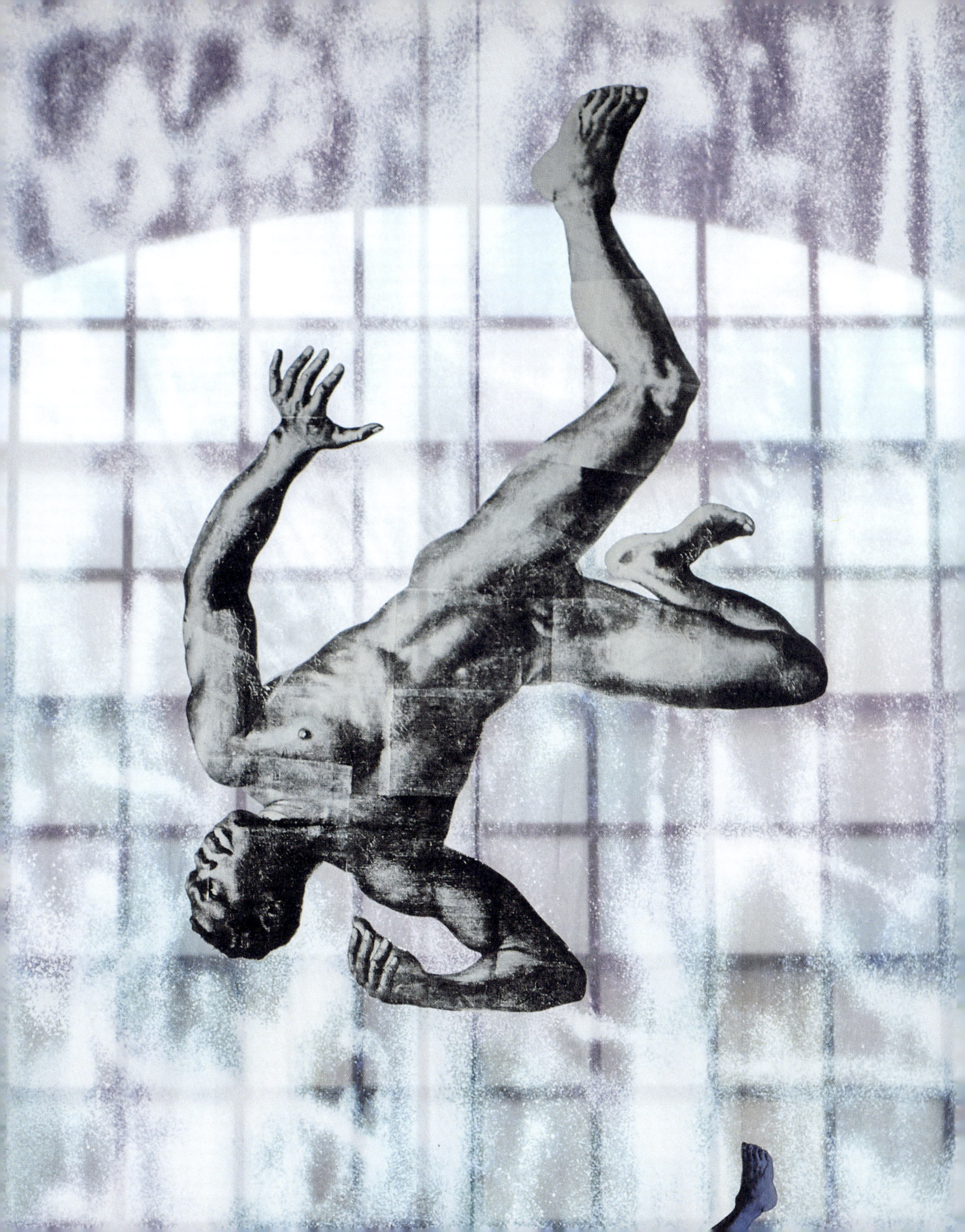

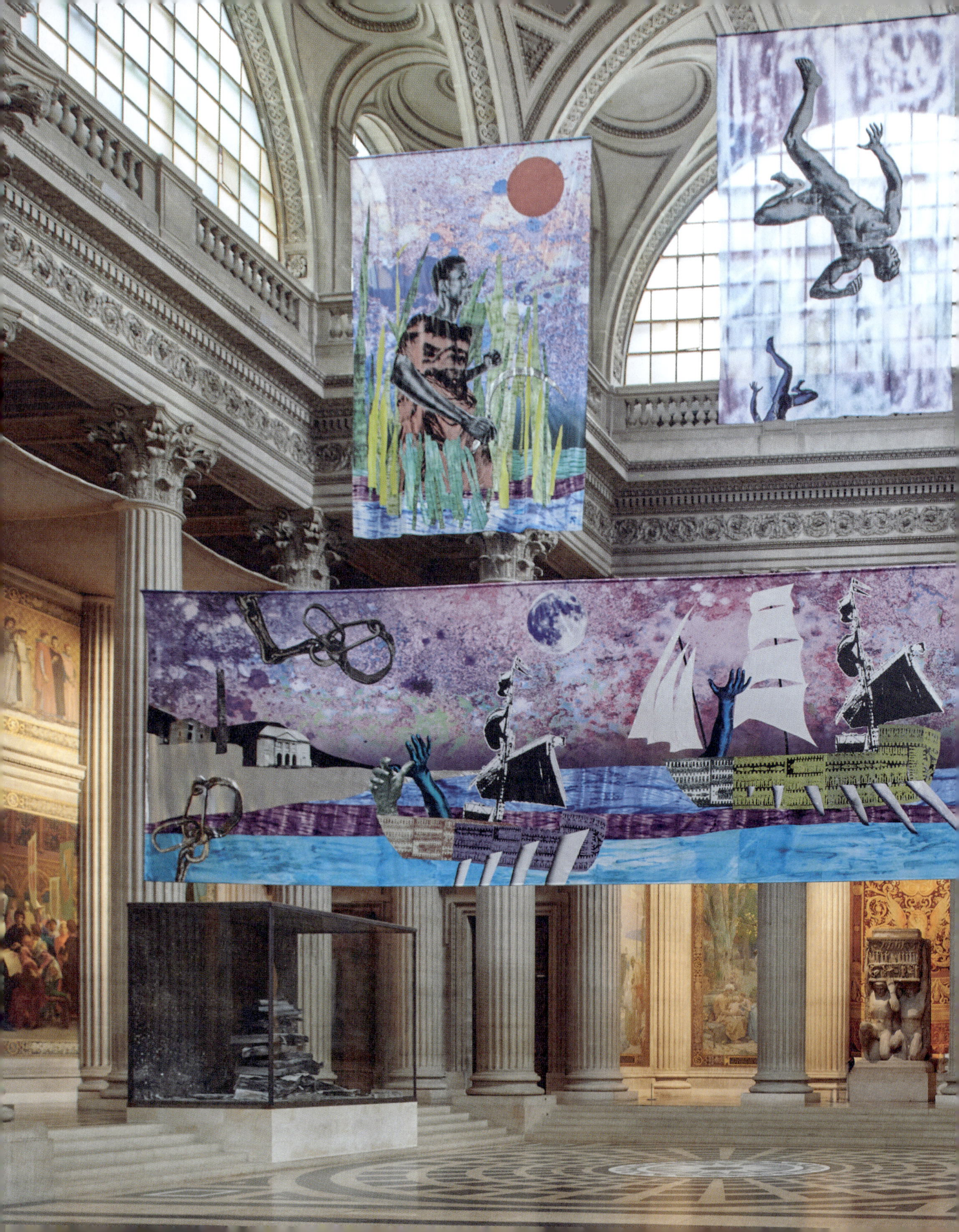

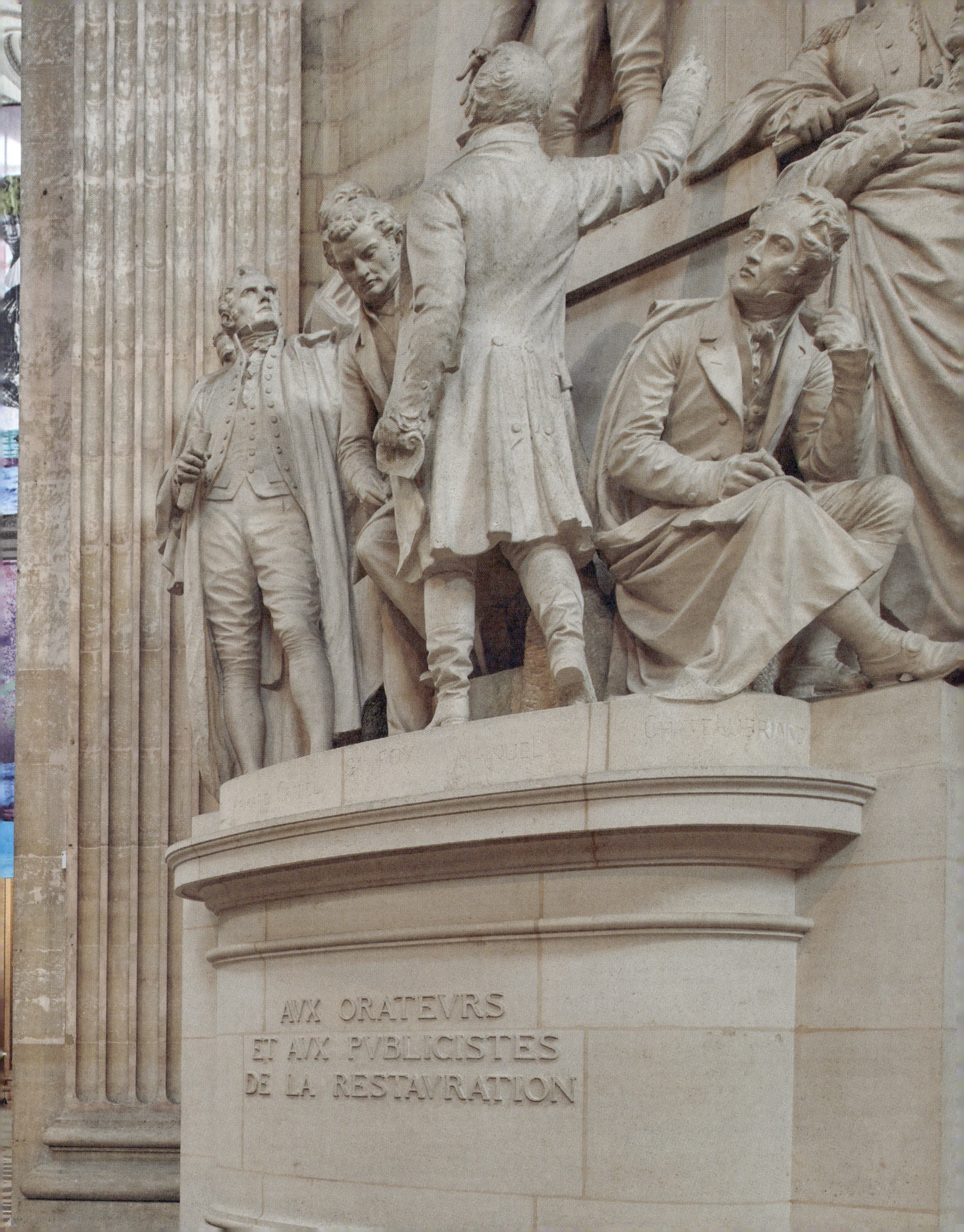
MANUEL
CHATEAUBRIAND
AVX ORATEVRS
ET AVX PVBLICISTES
DE LA RESTAVRATION

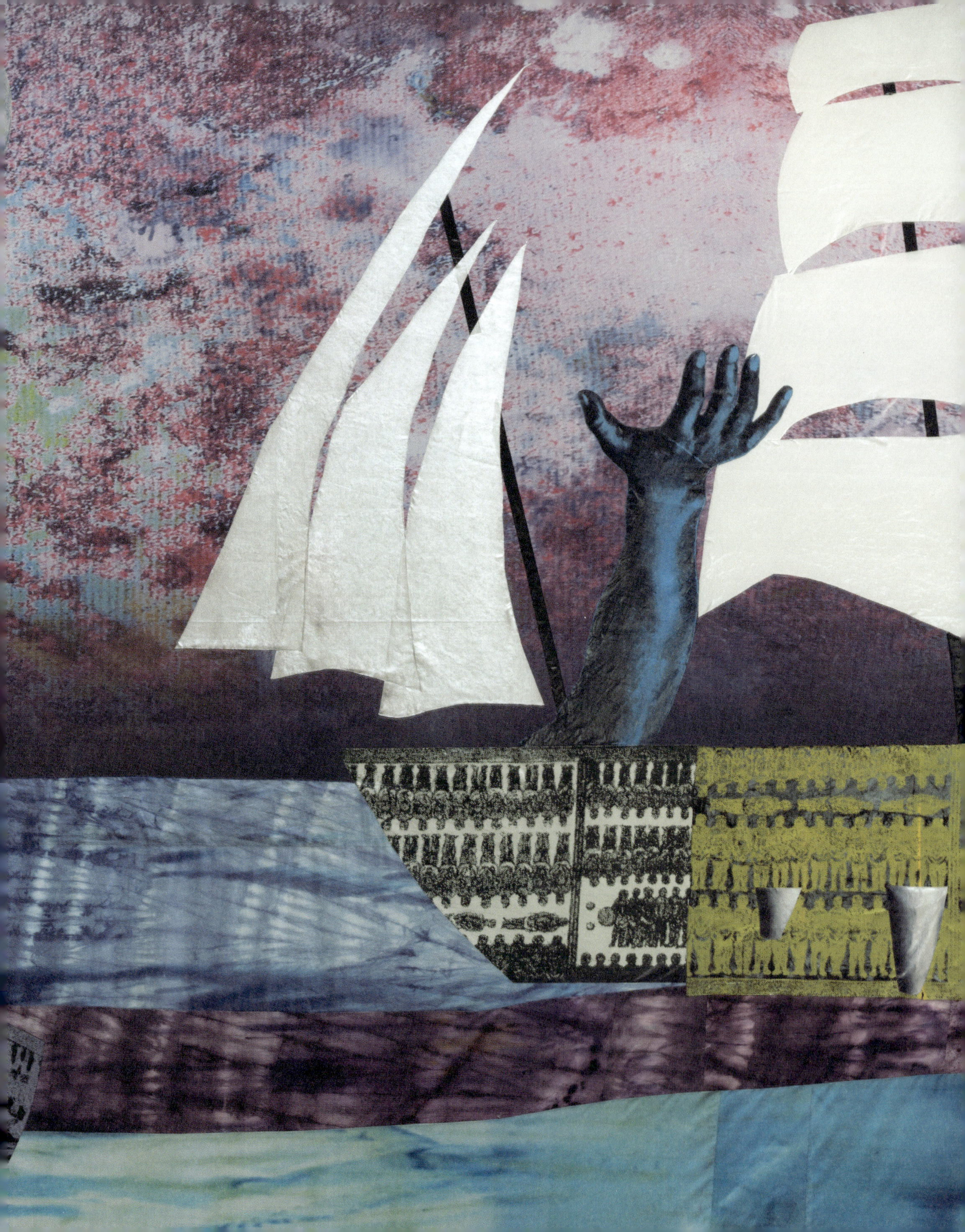

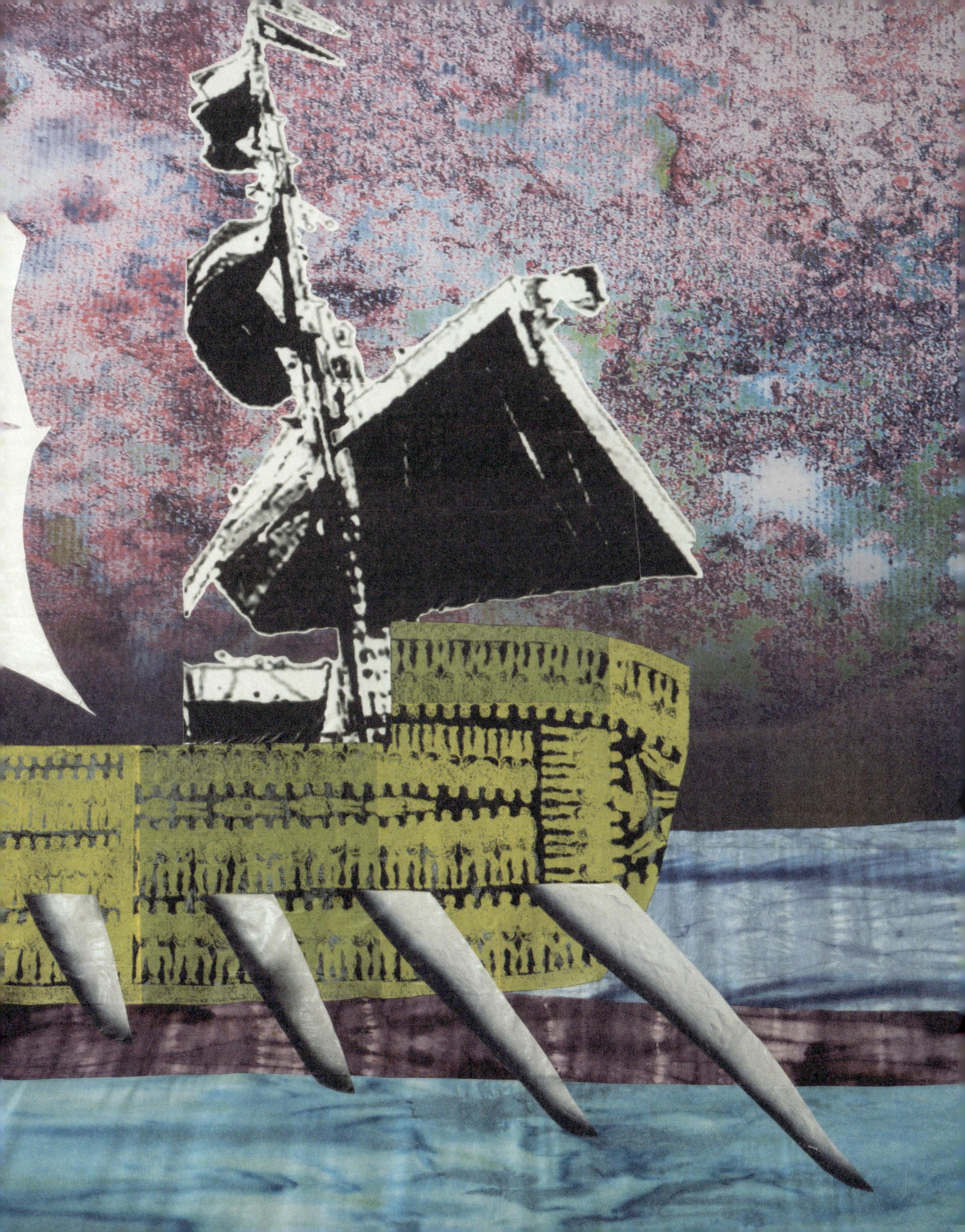

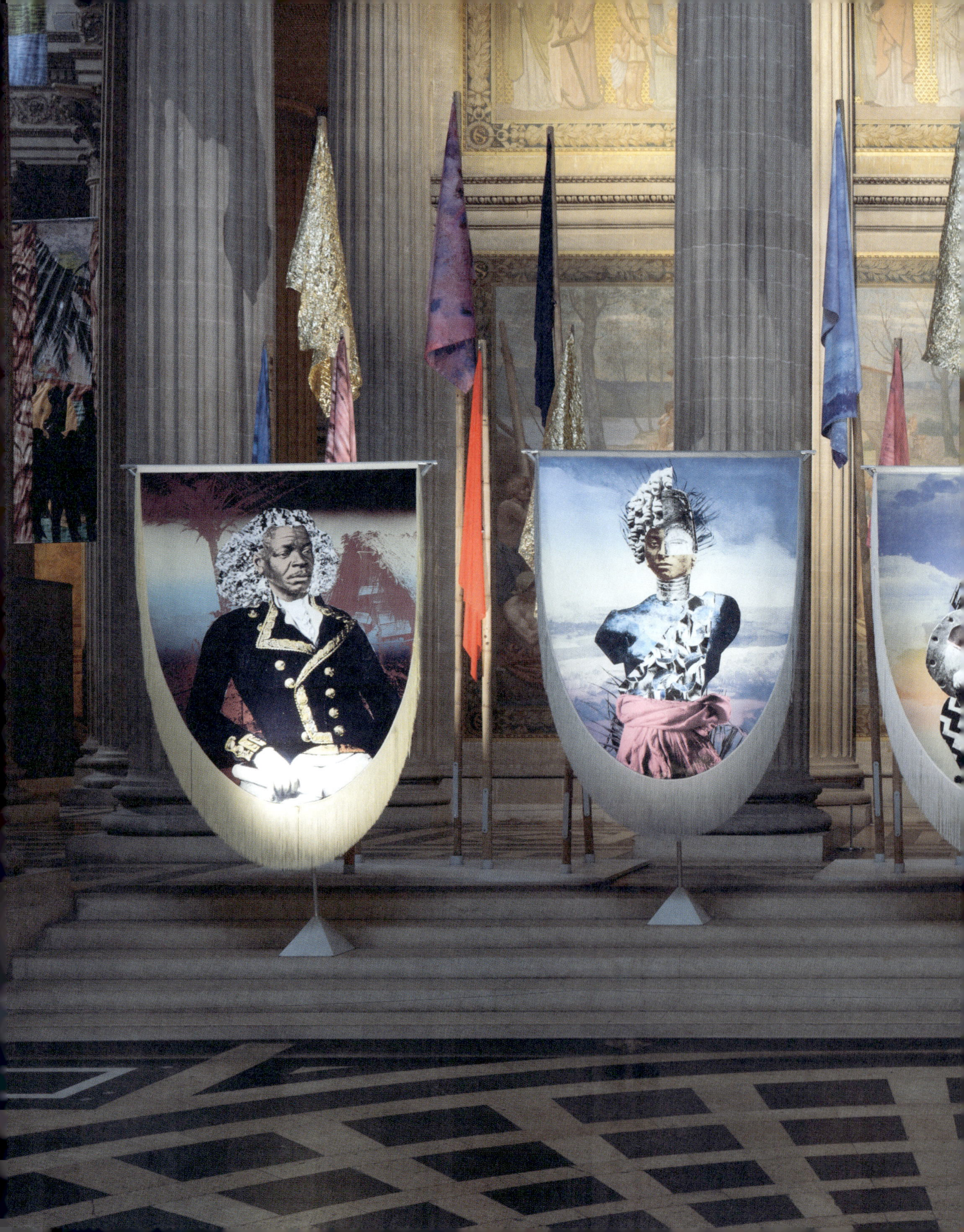

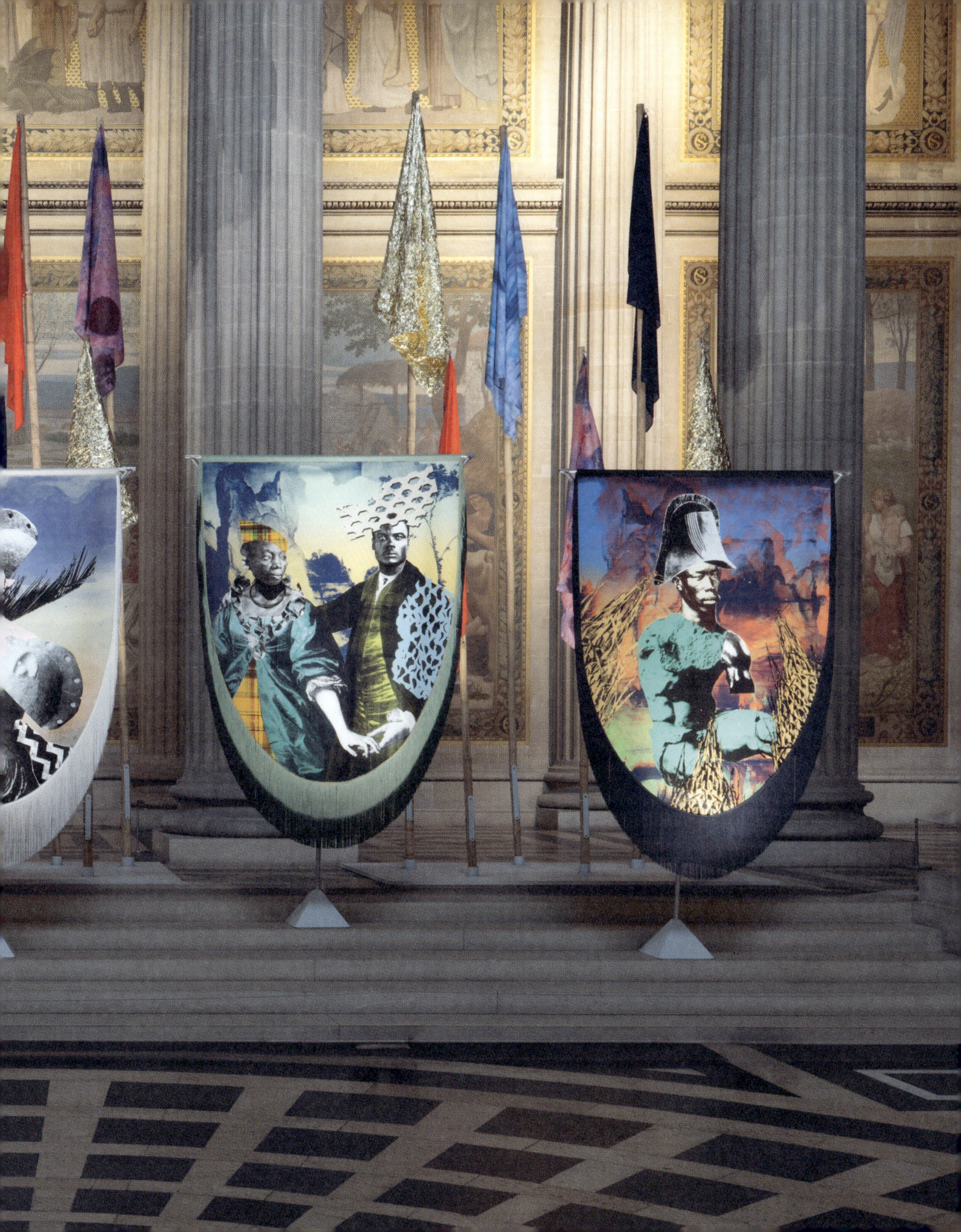

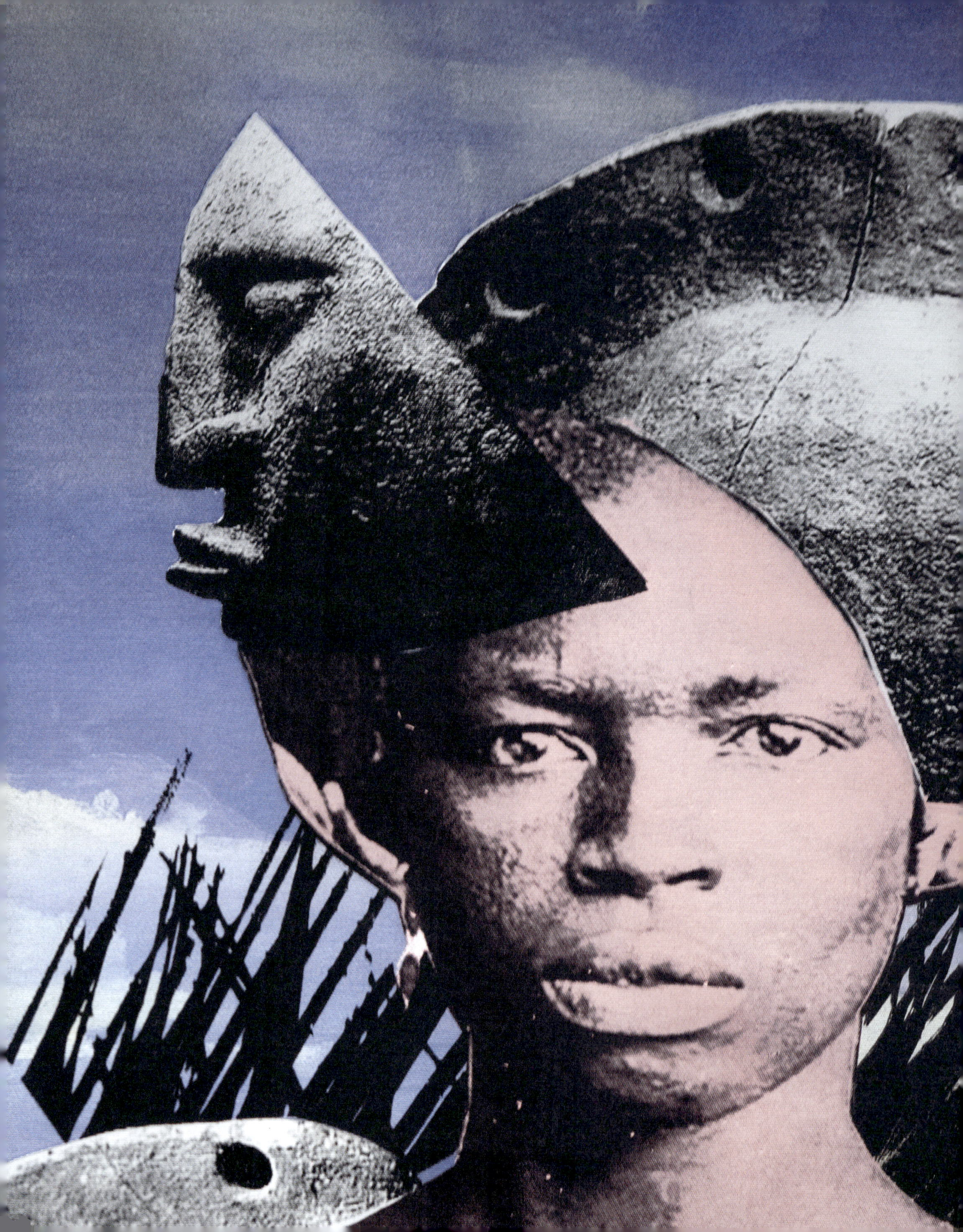

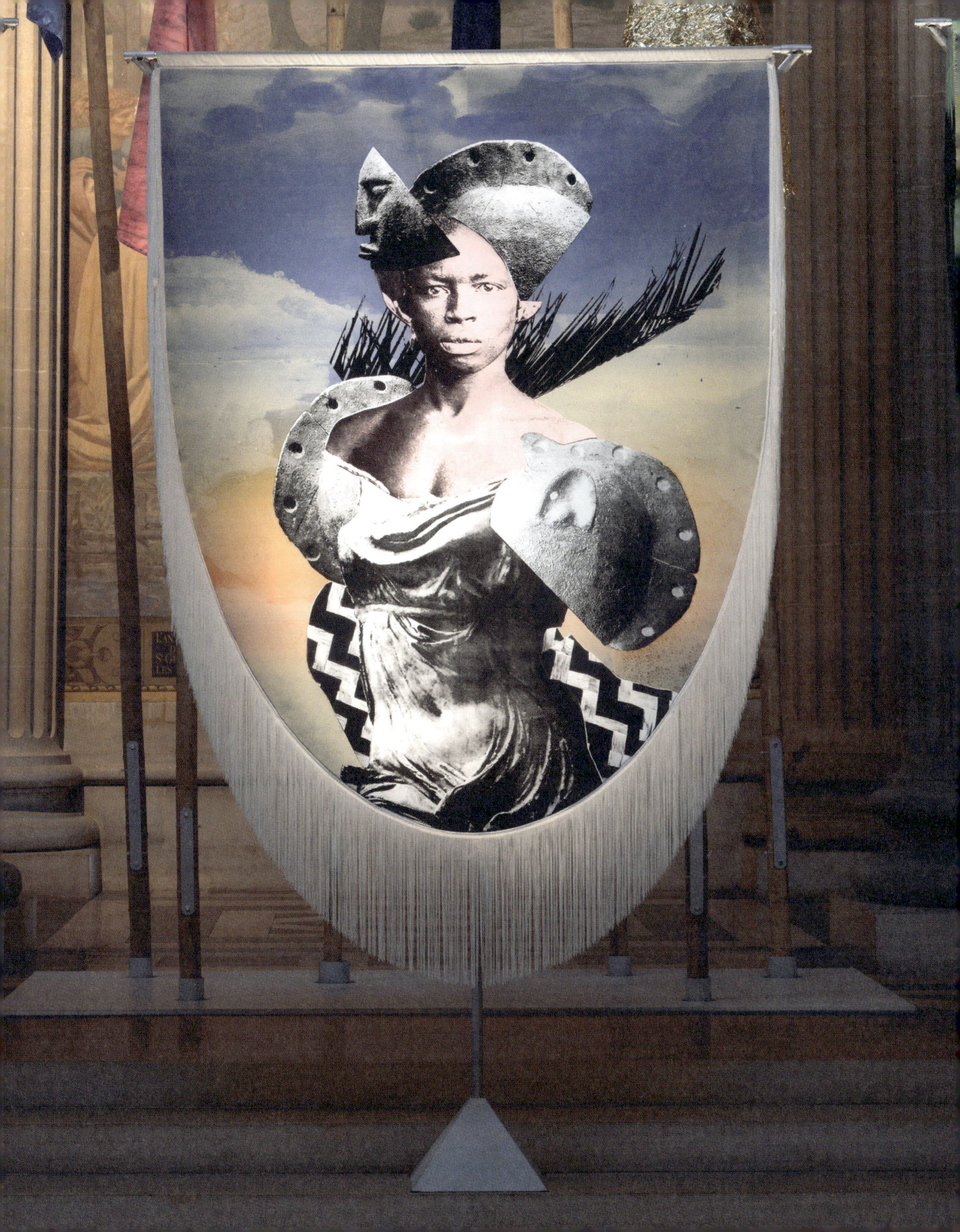

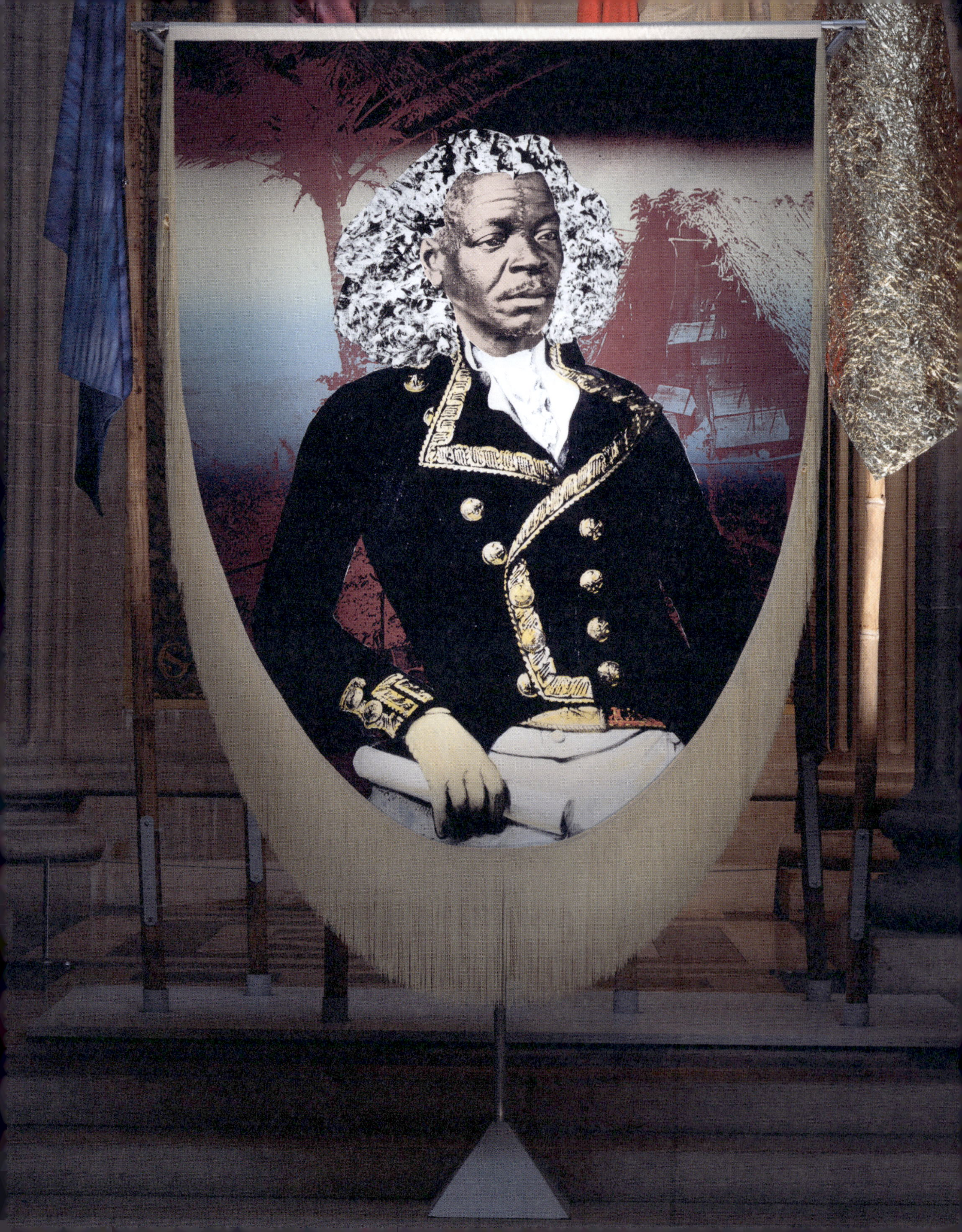

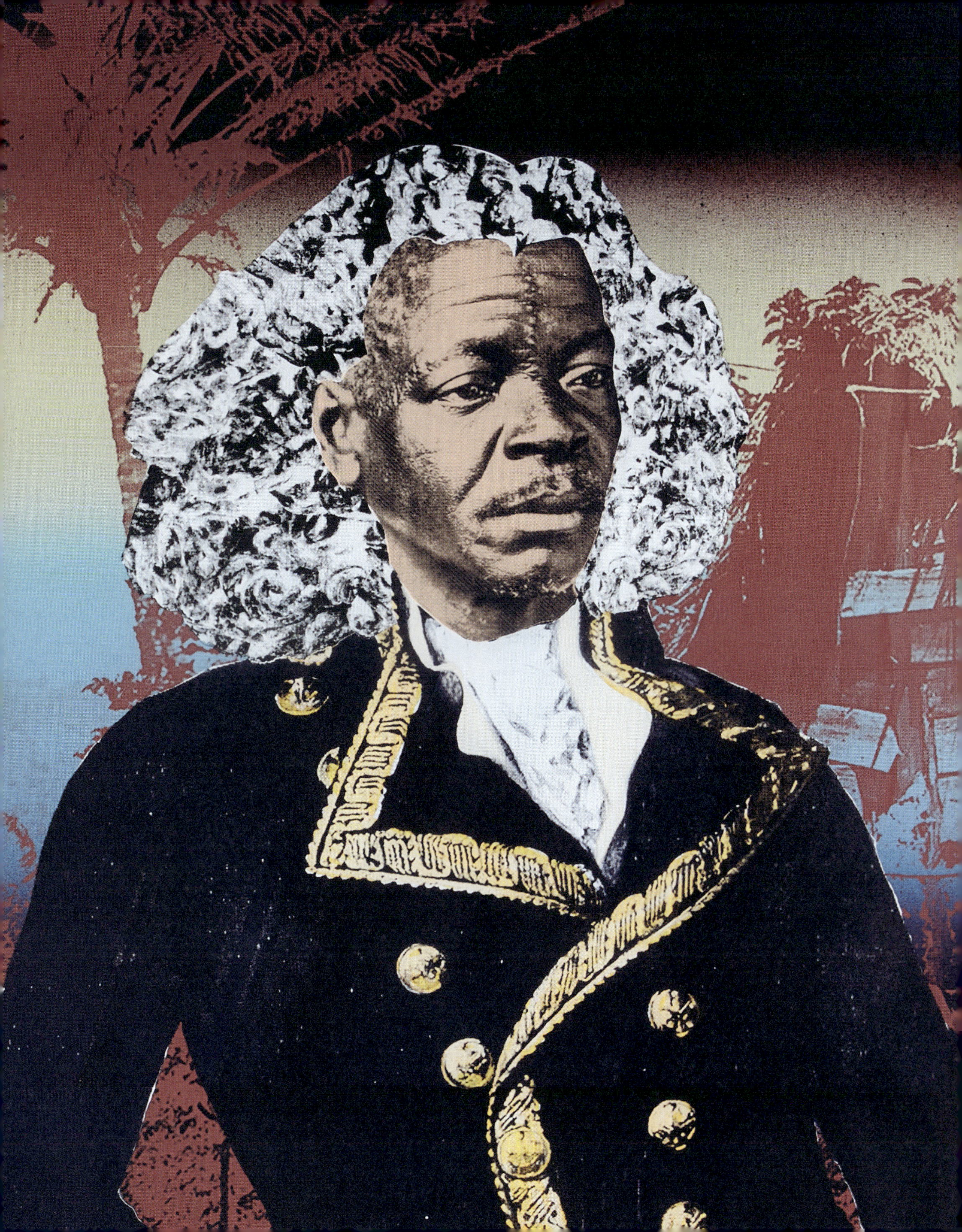

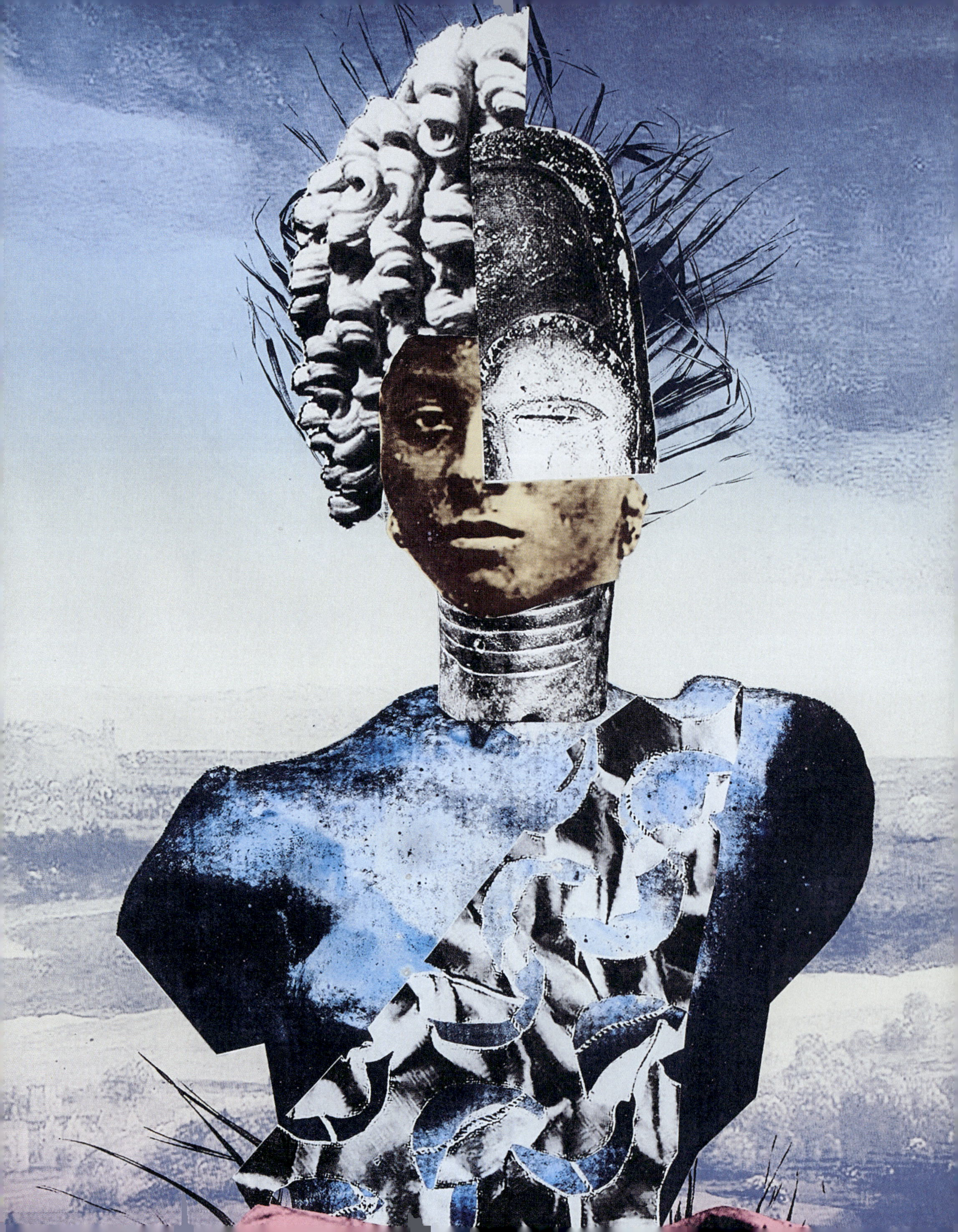

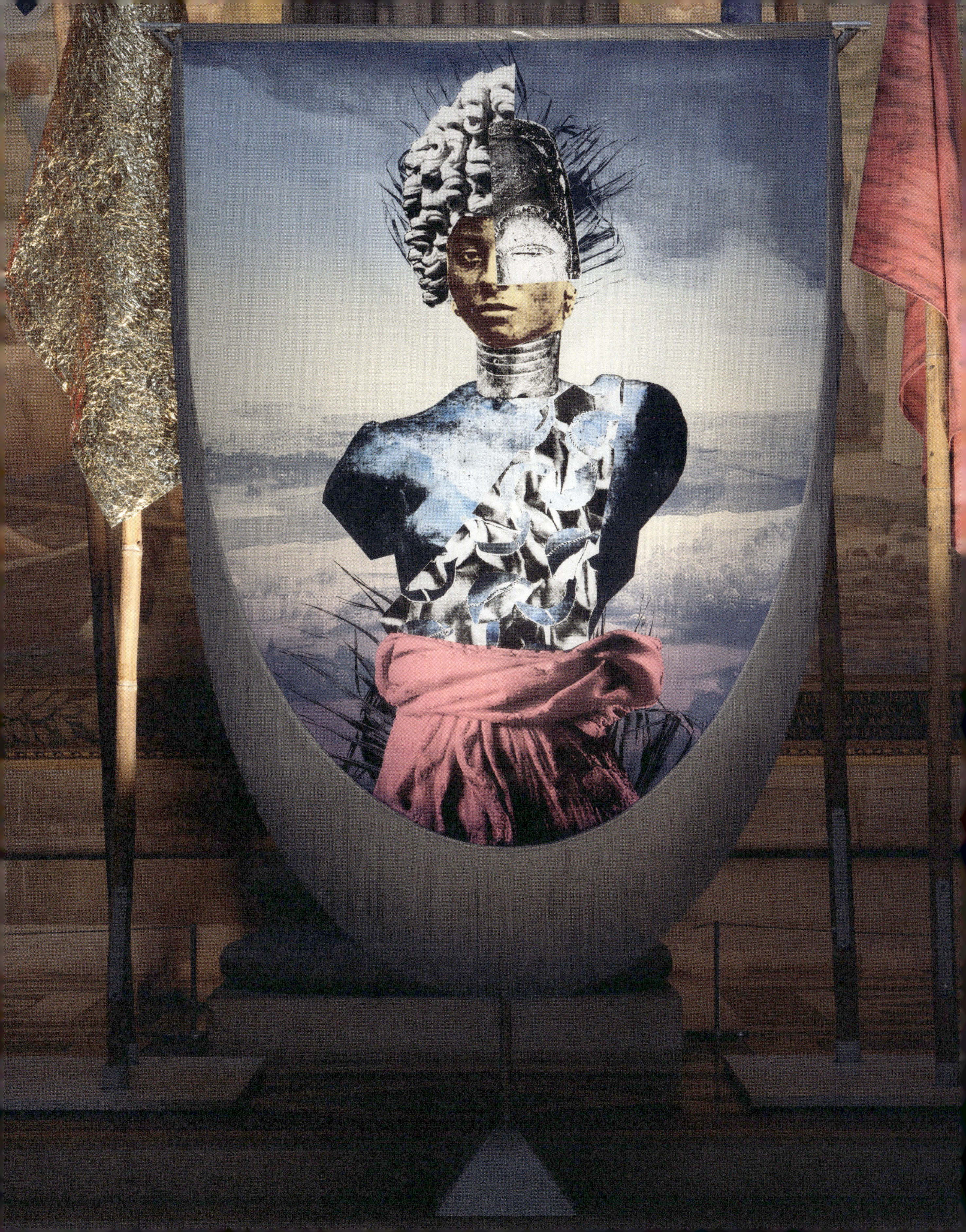

p. 69 *Anchaing and Héva*, 2023
p. 70 *Joseph Ignace* (detail), 2023
p. 71 *Joseph Ignace*, 2023

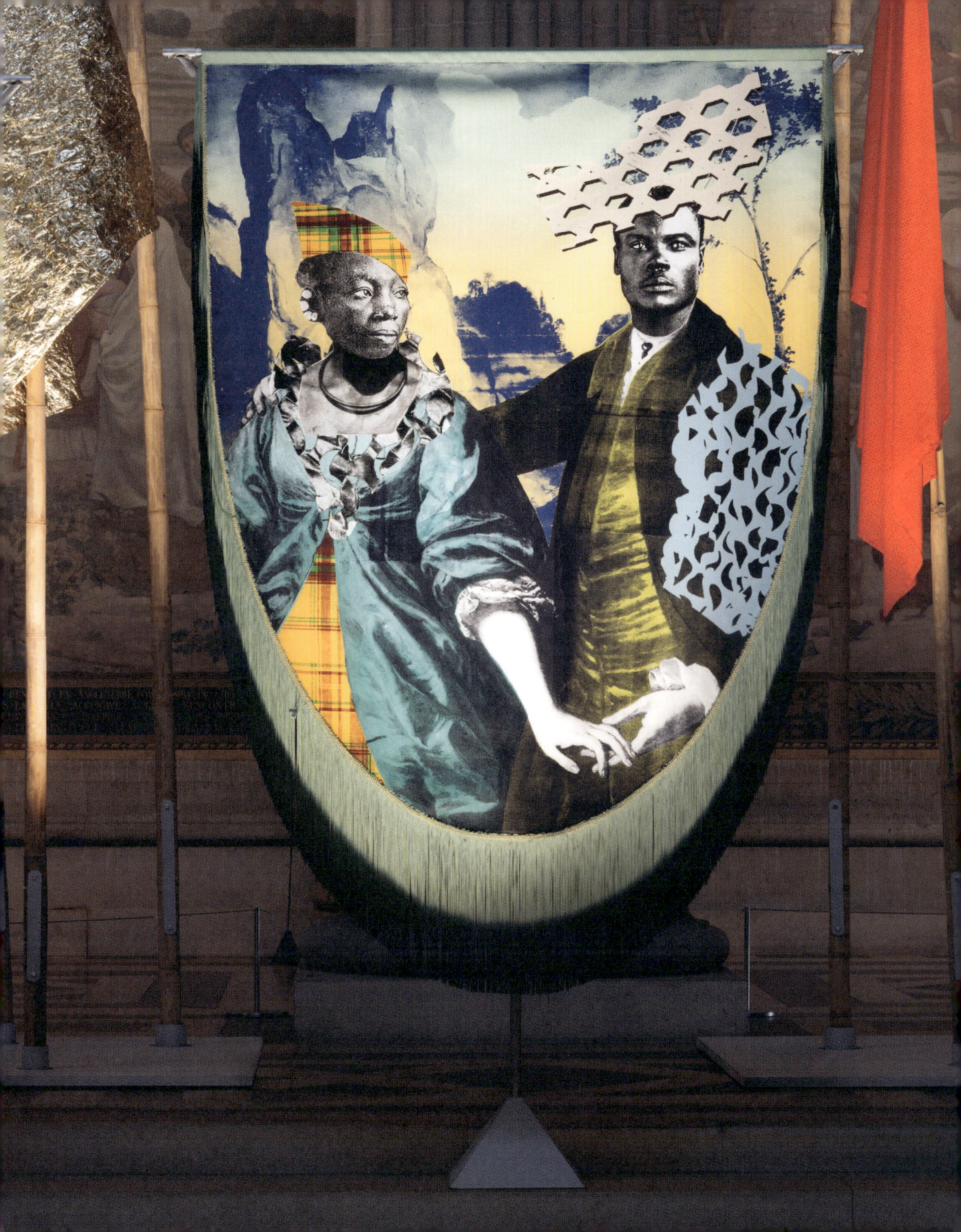

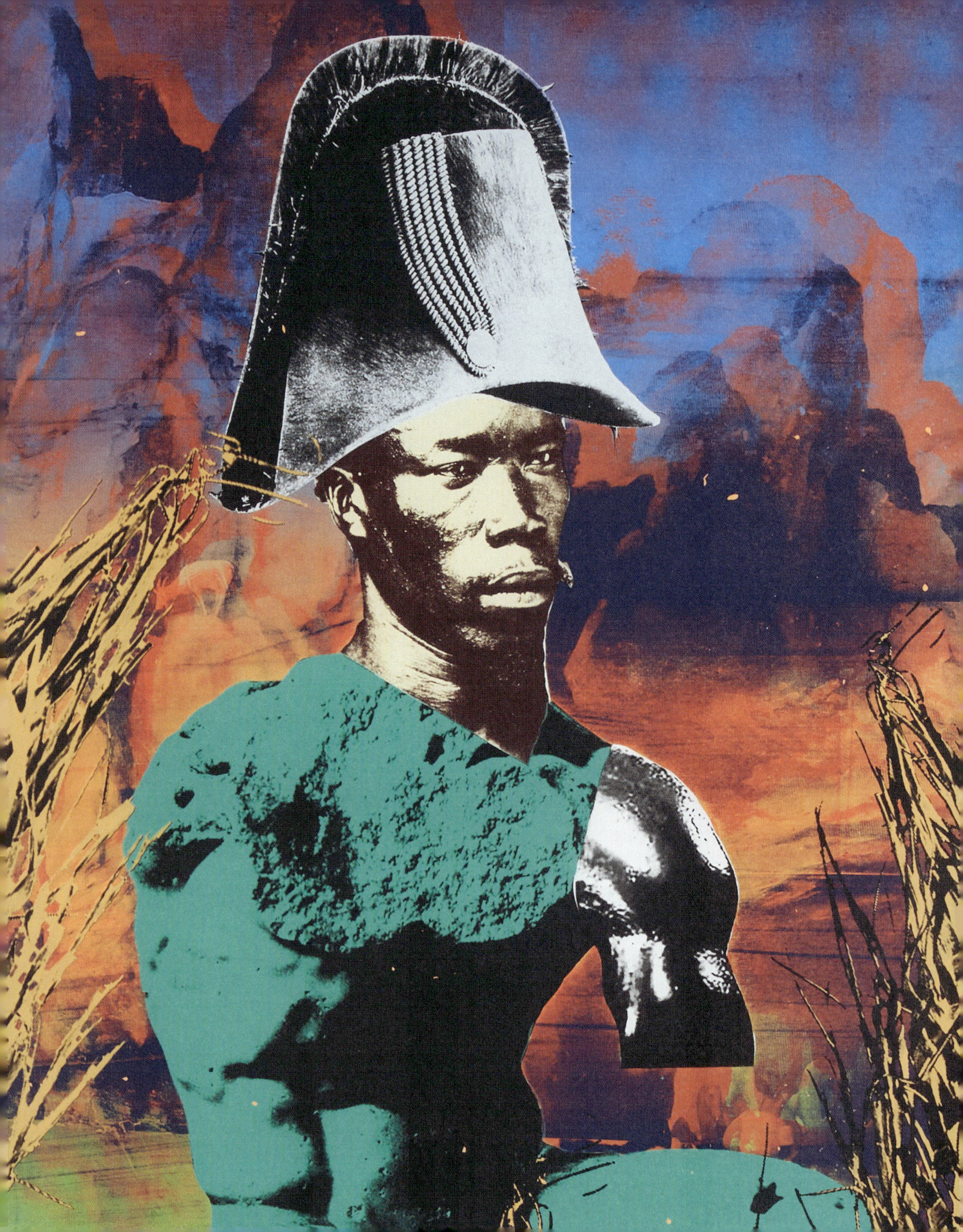

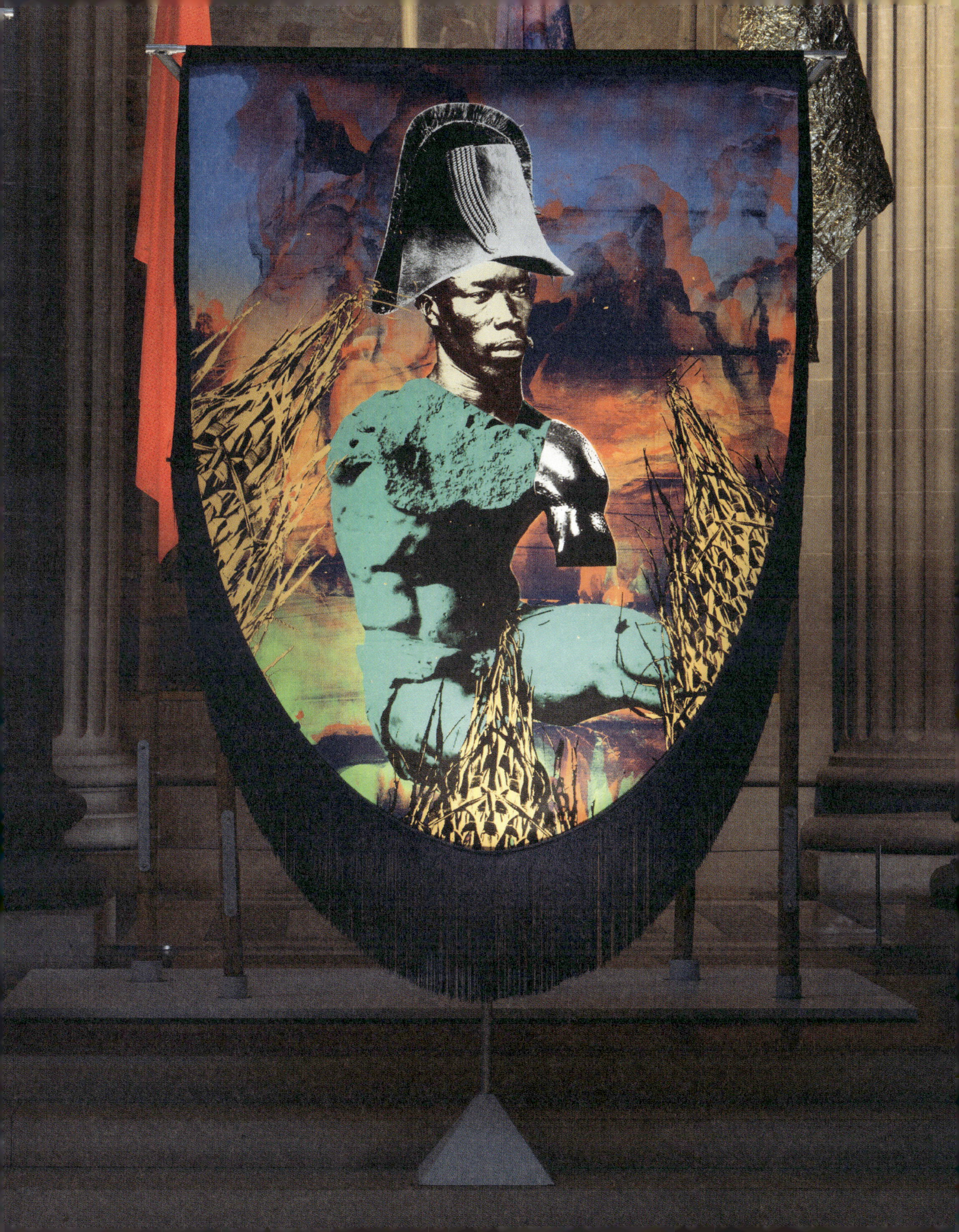

p. 73 *Untitled* (detail), 2023

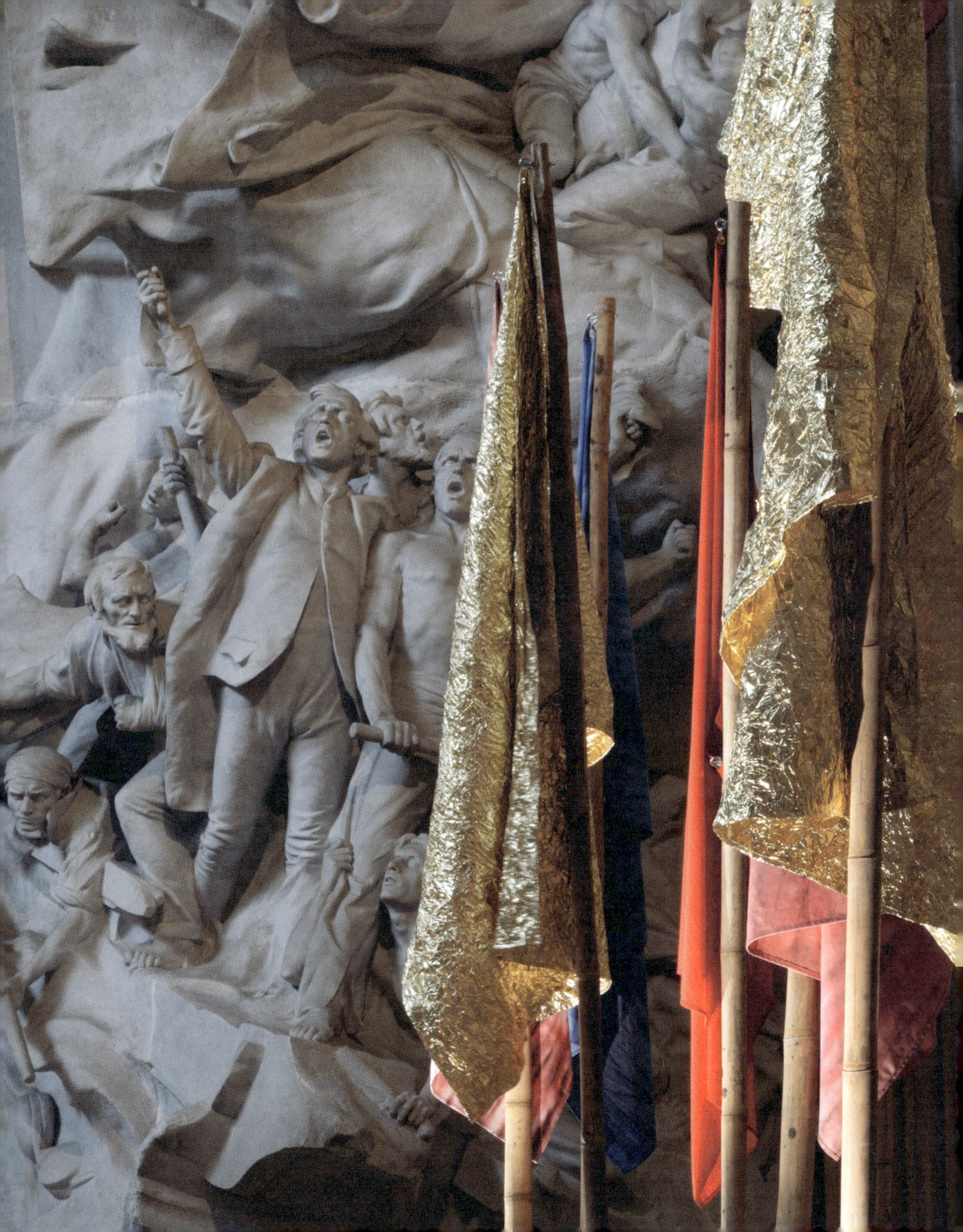

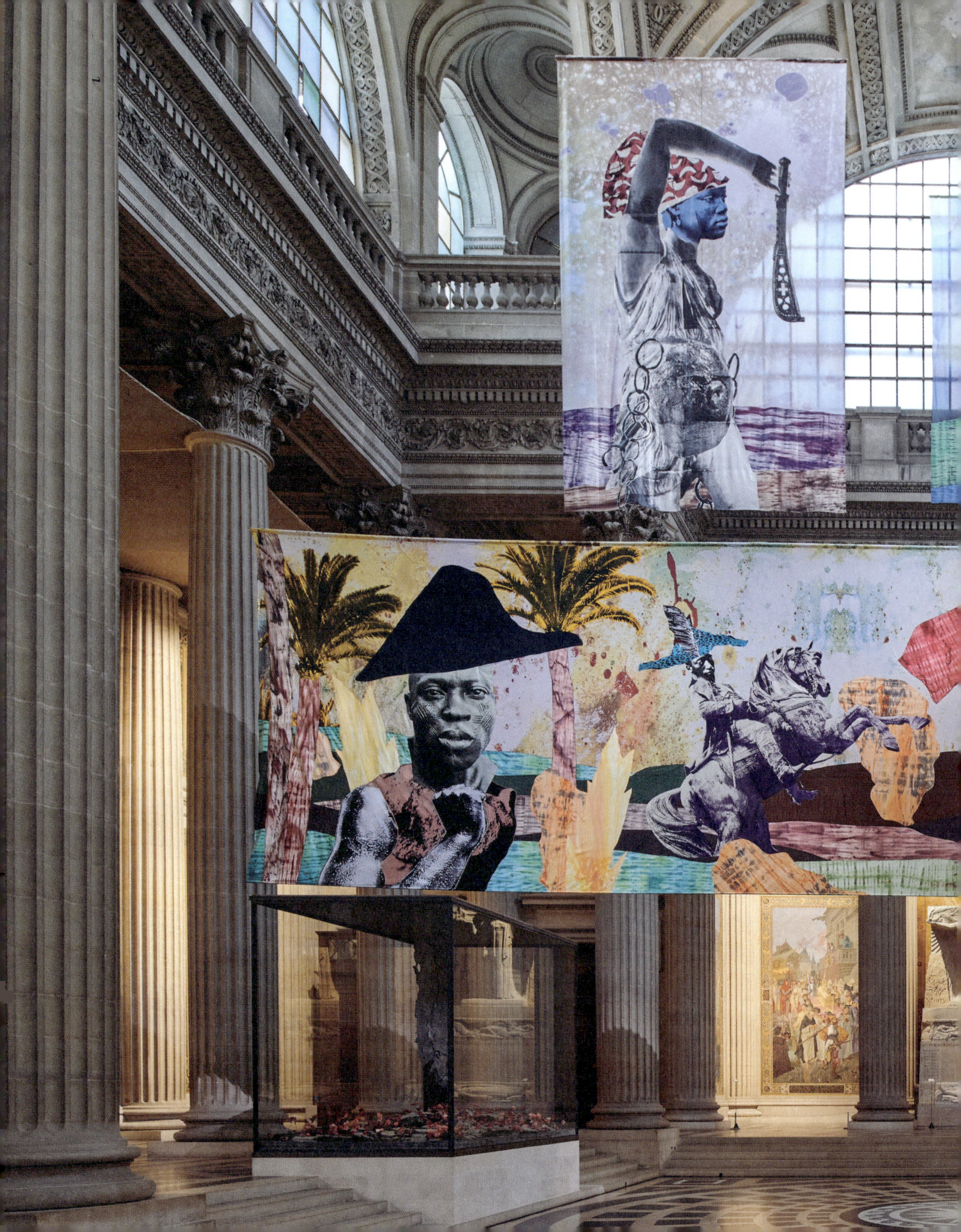

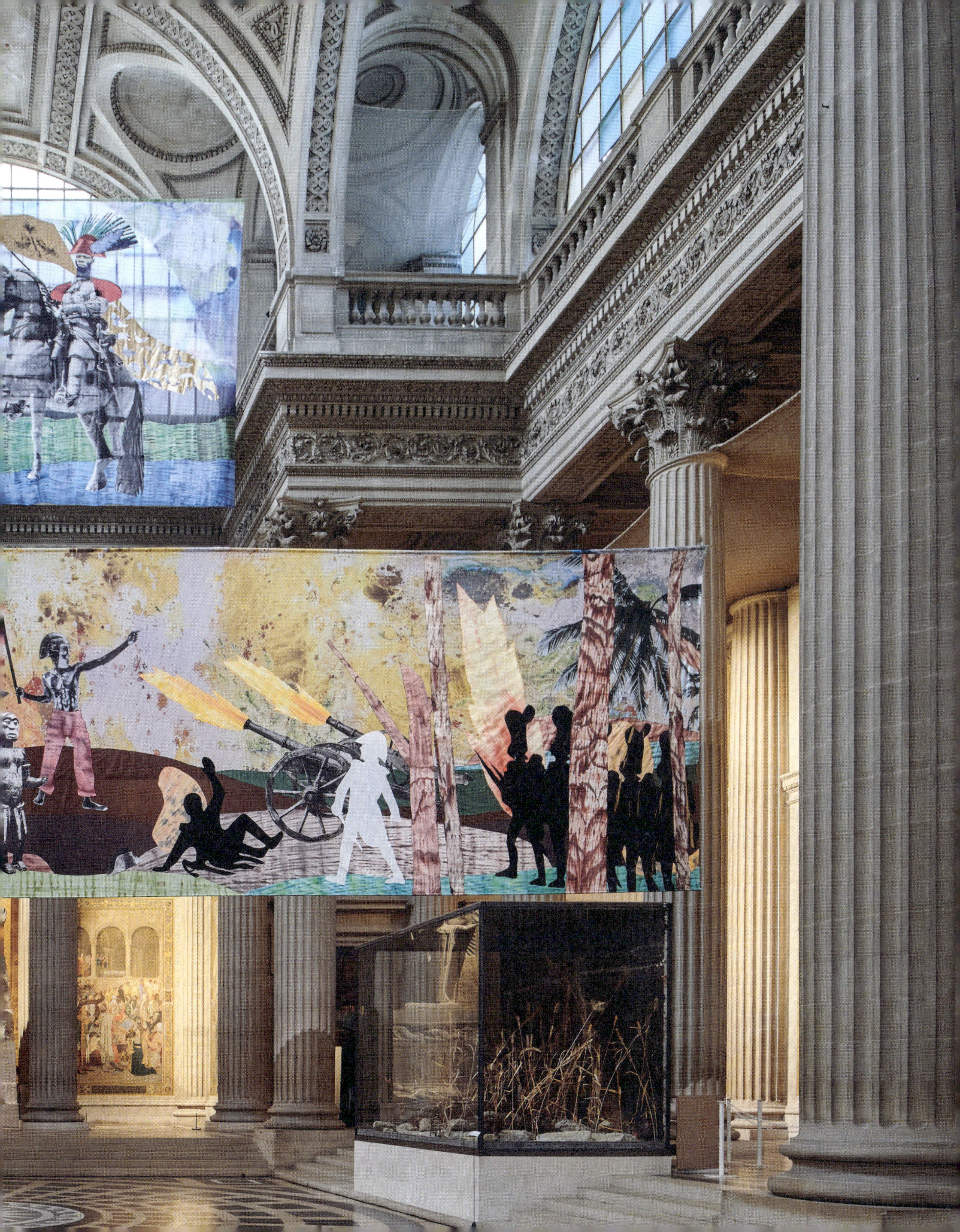

p. 78-79 *Toussaint's Triumph*, 2023

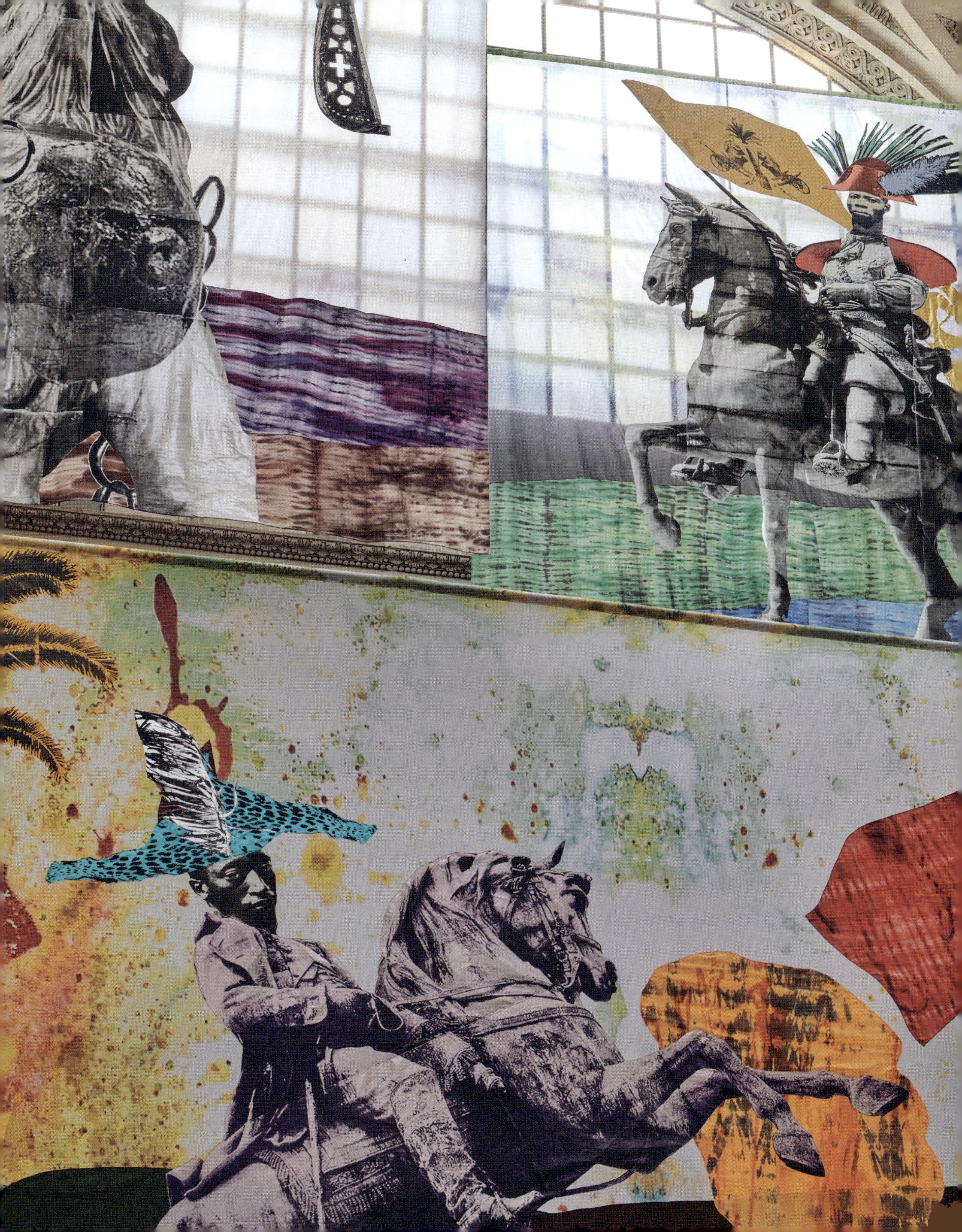

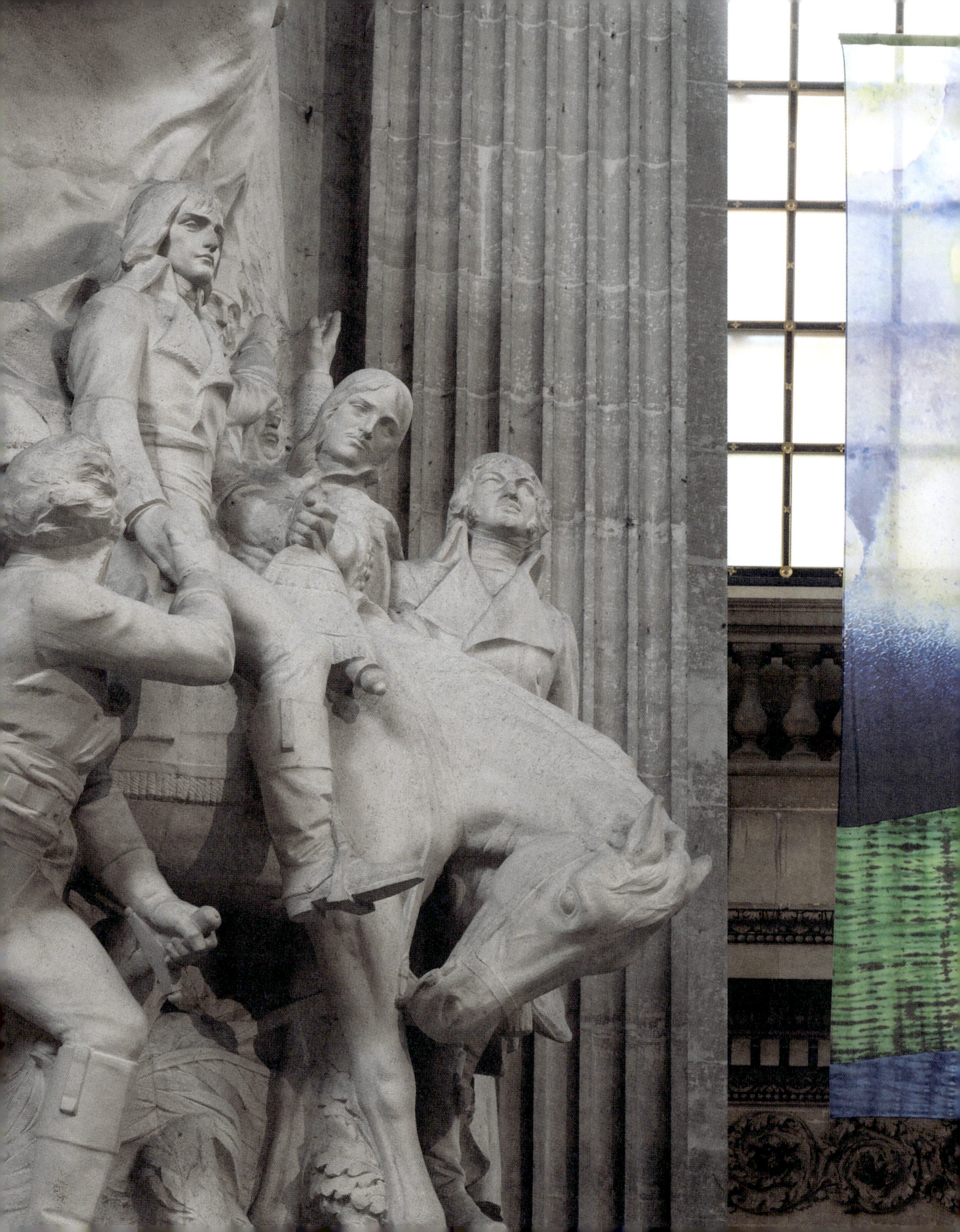

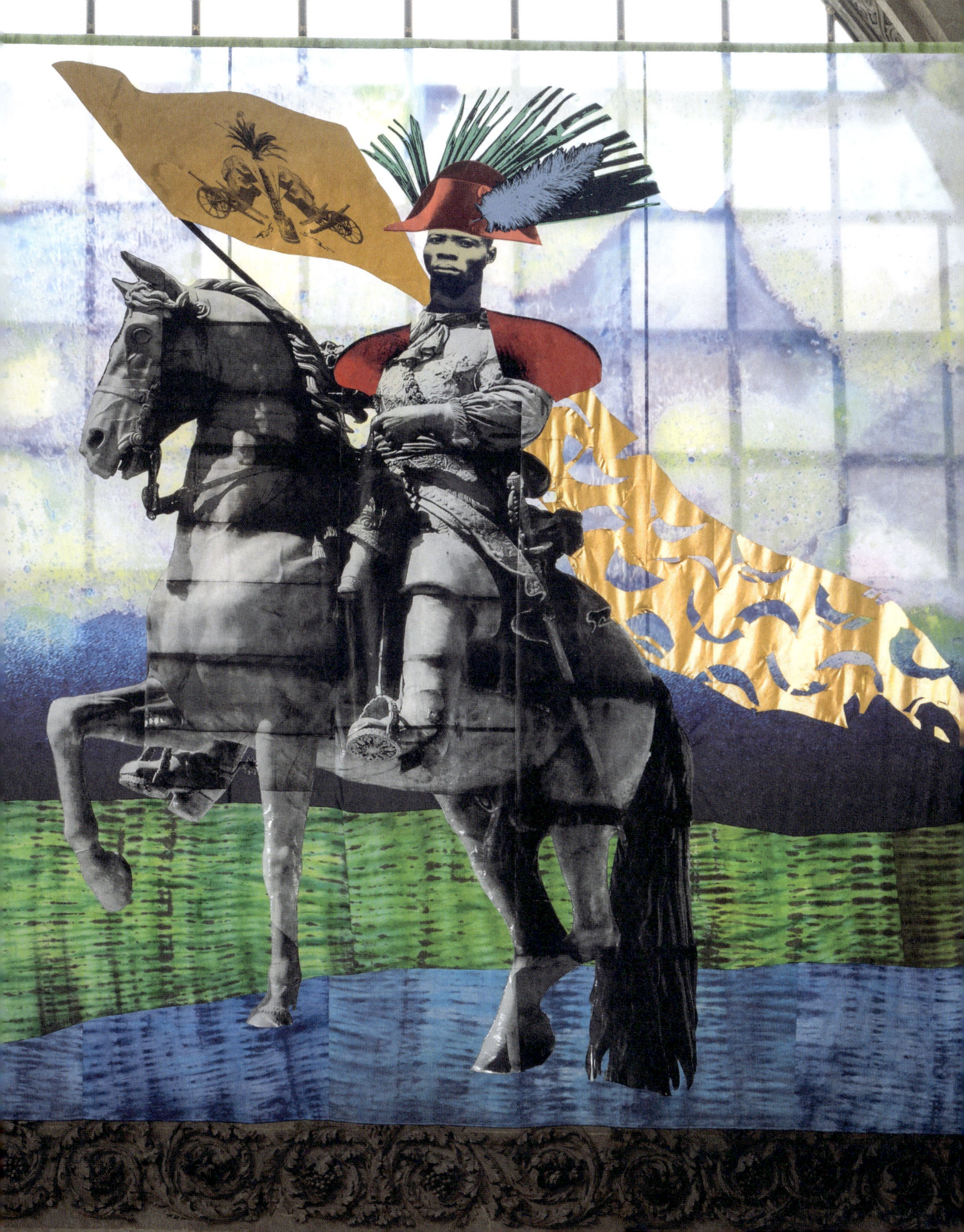

p. 81 *Toussaint's Triumph* (detail), 2023

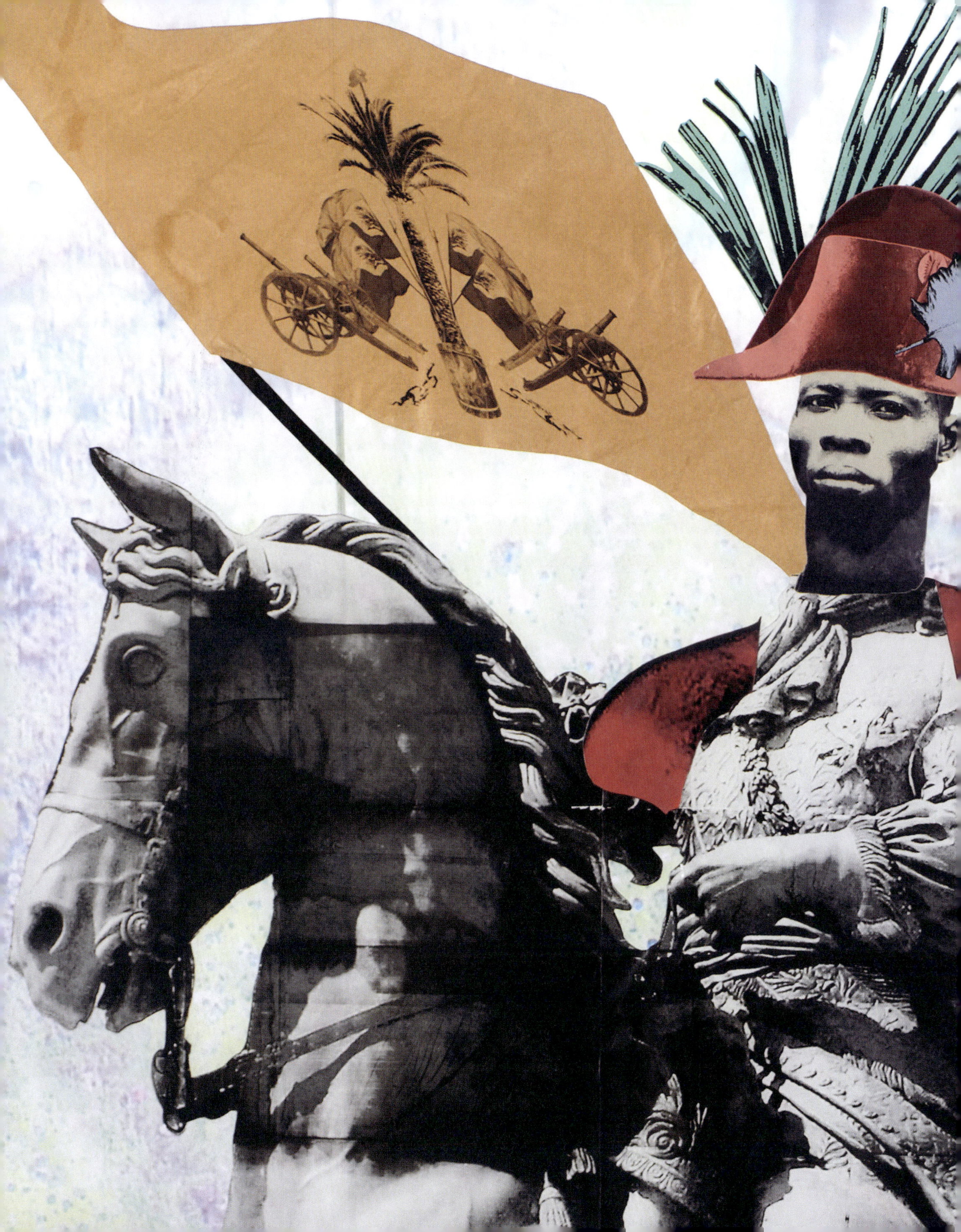

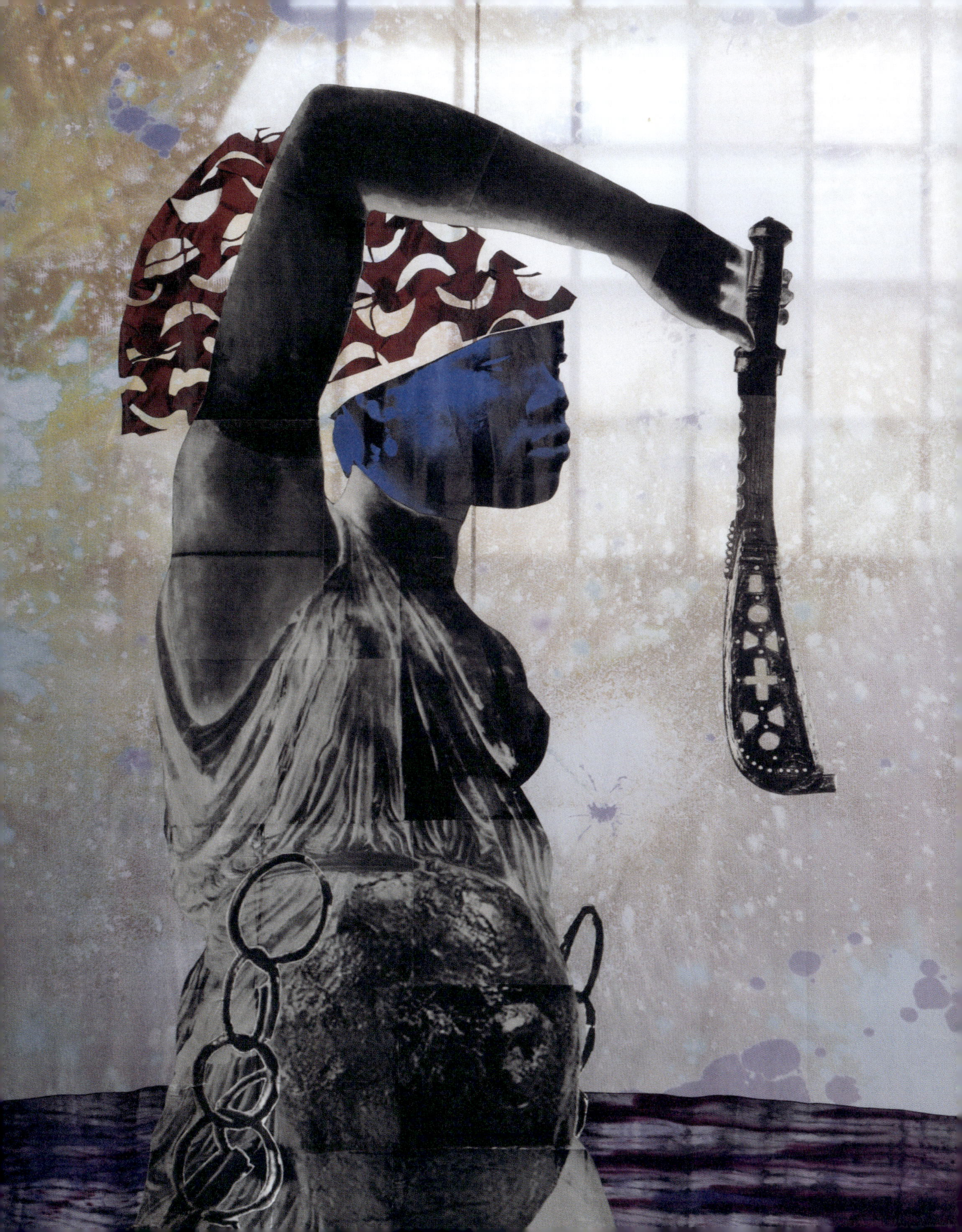

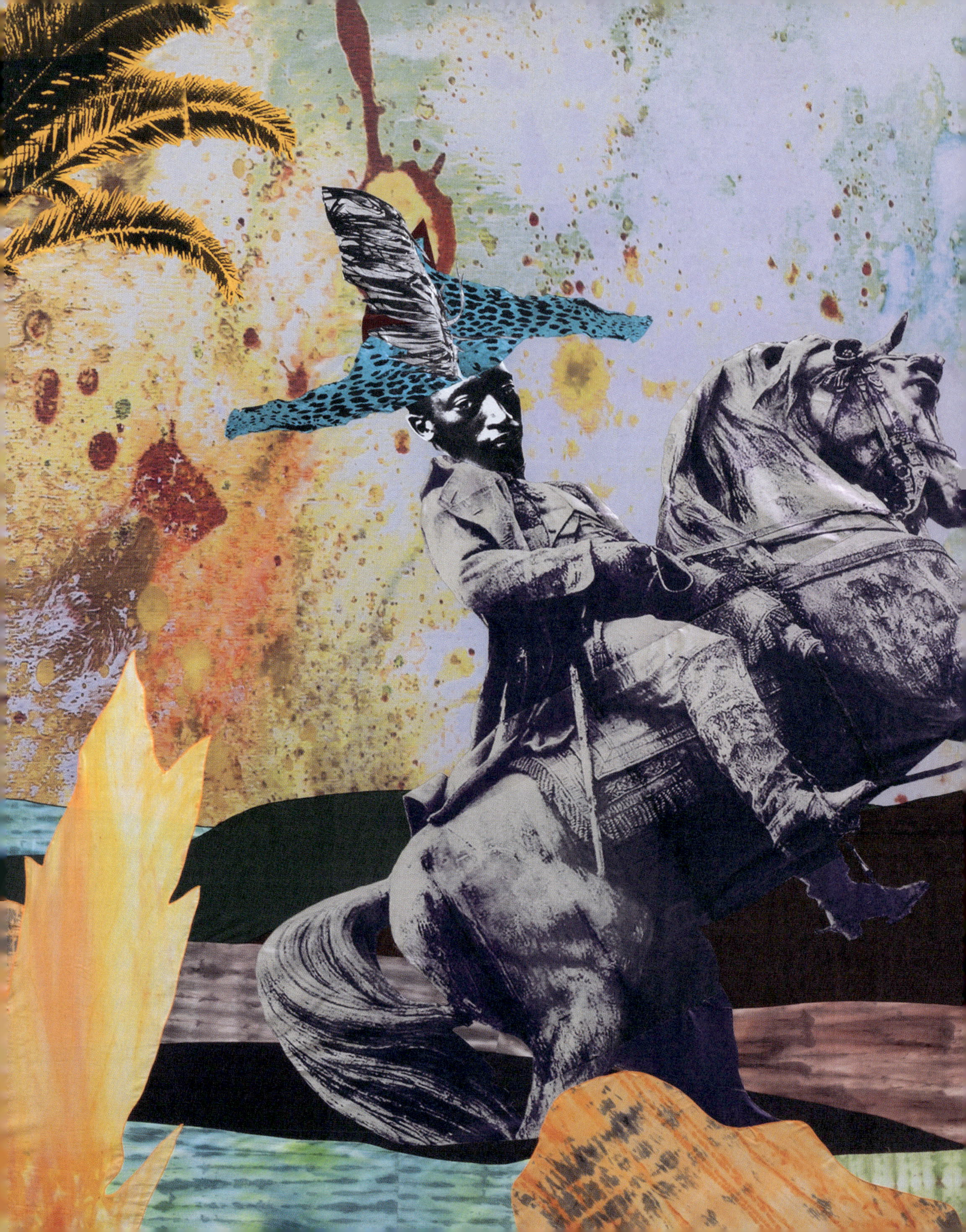

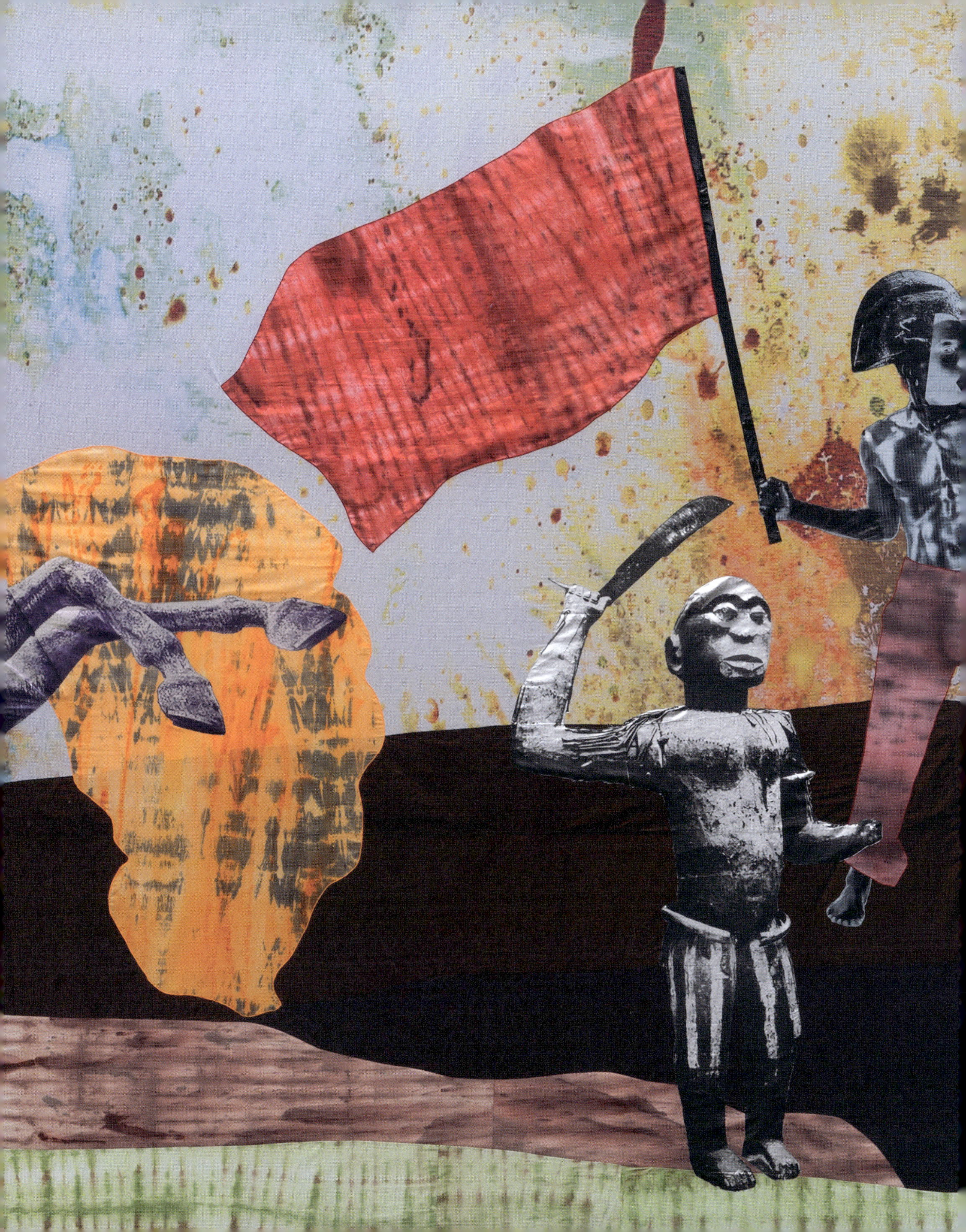

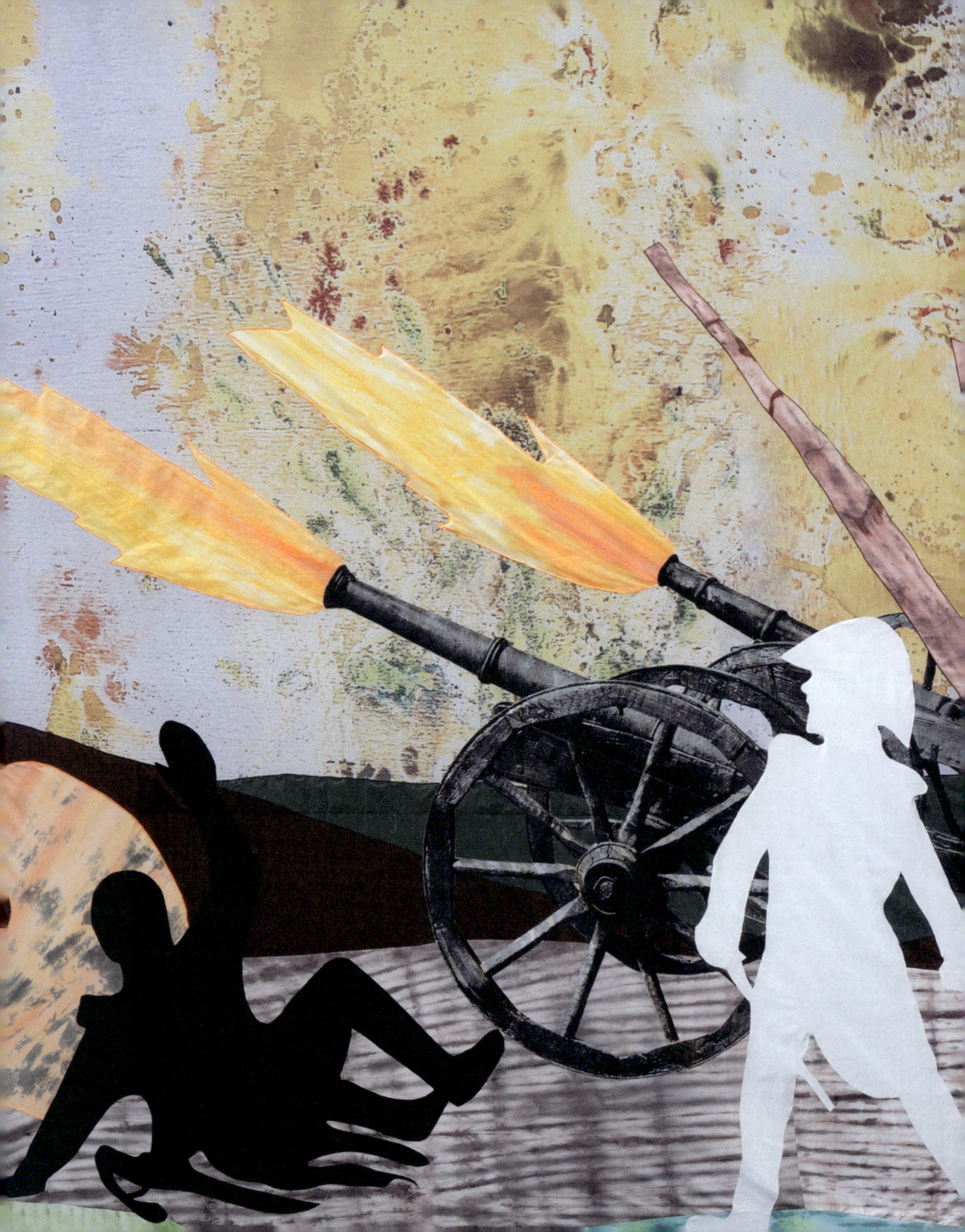

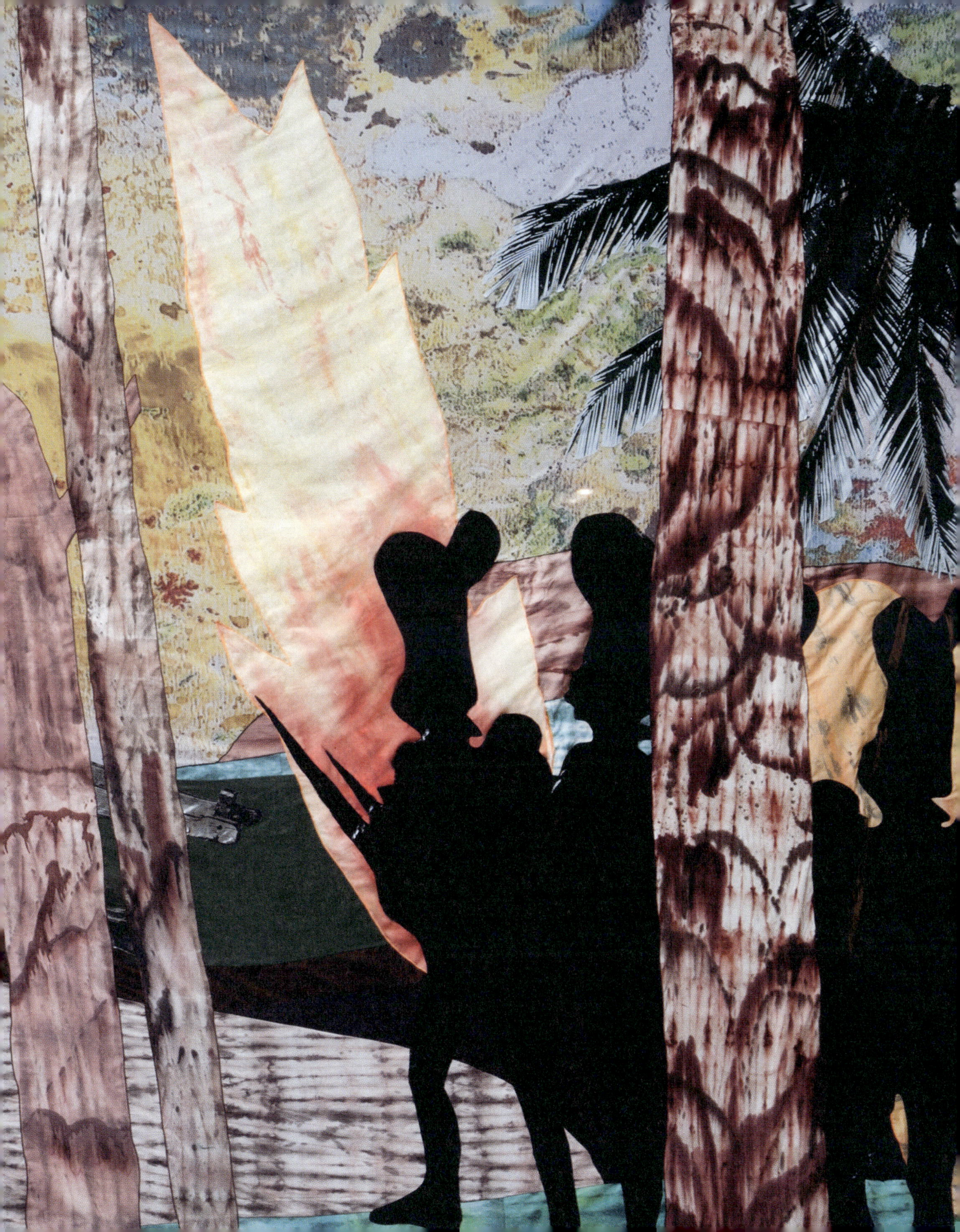

p. 89 *The Battle of Vertières* (detail), 2023

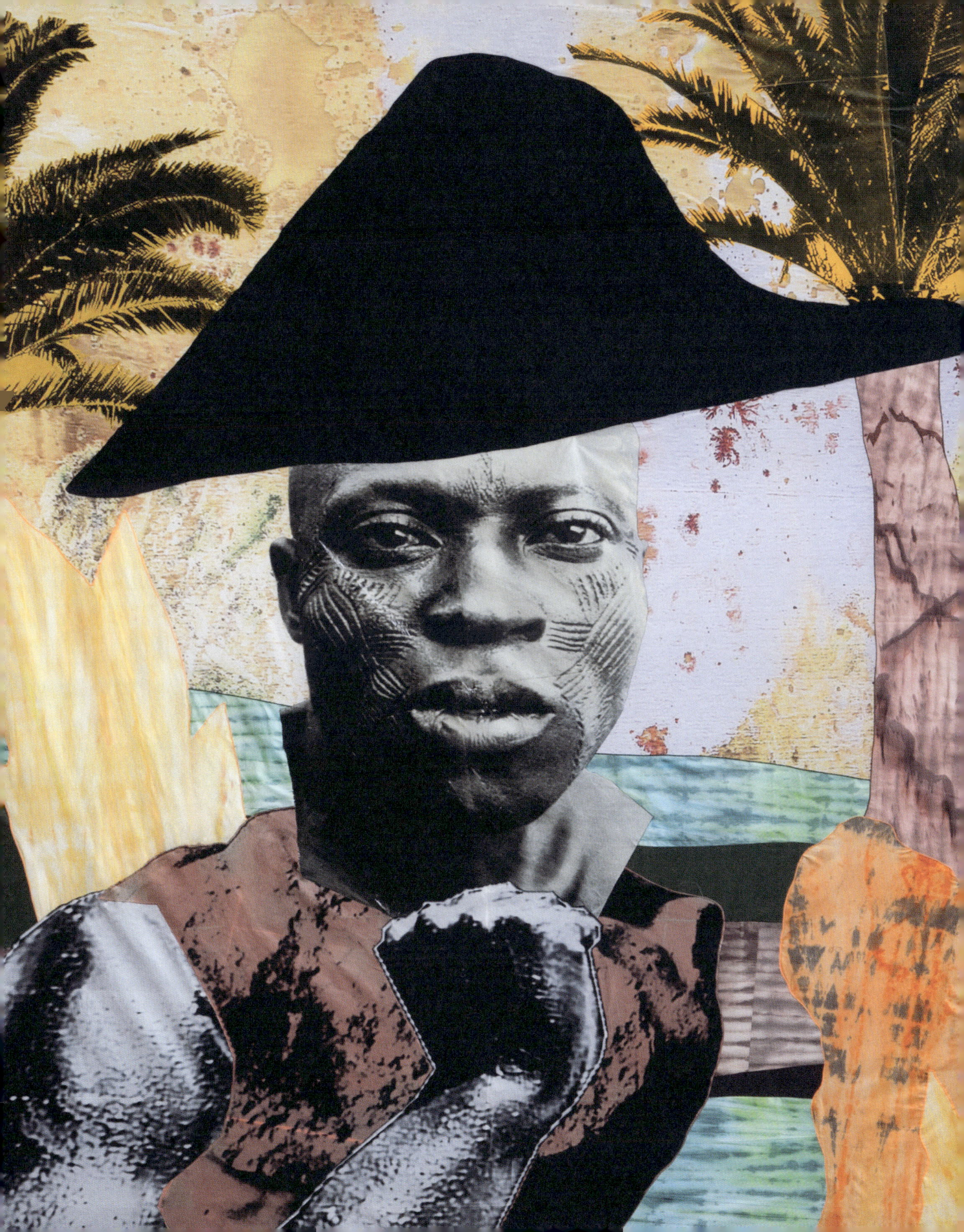

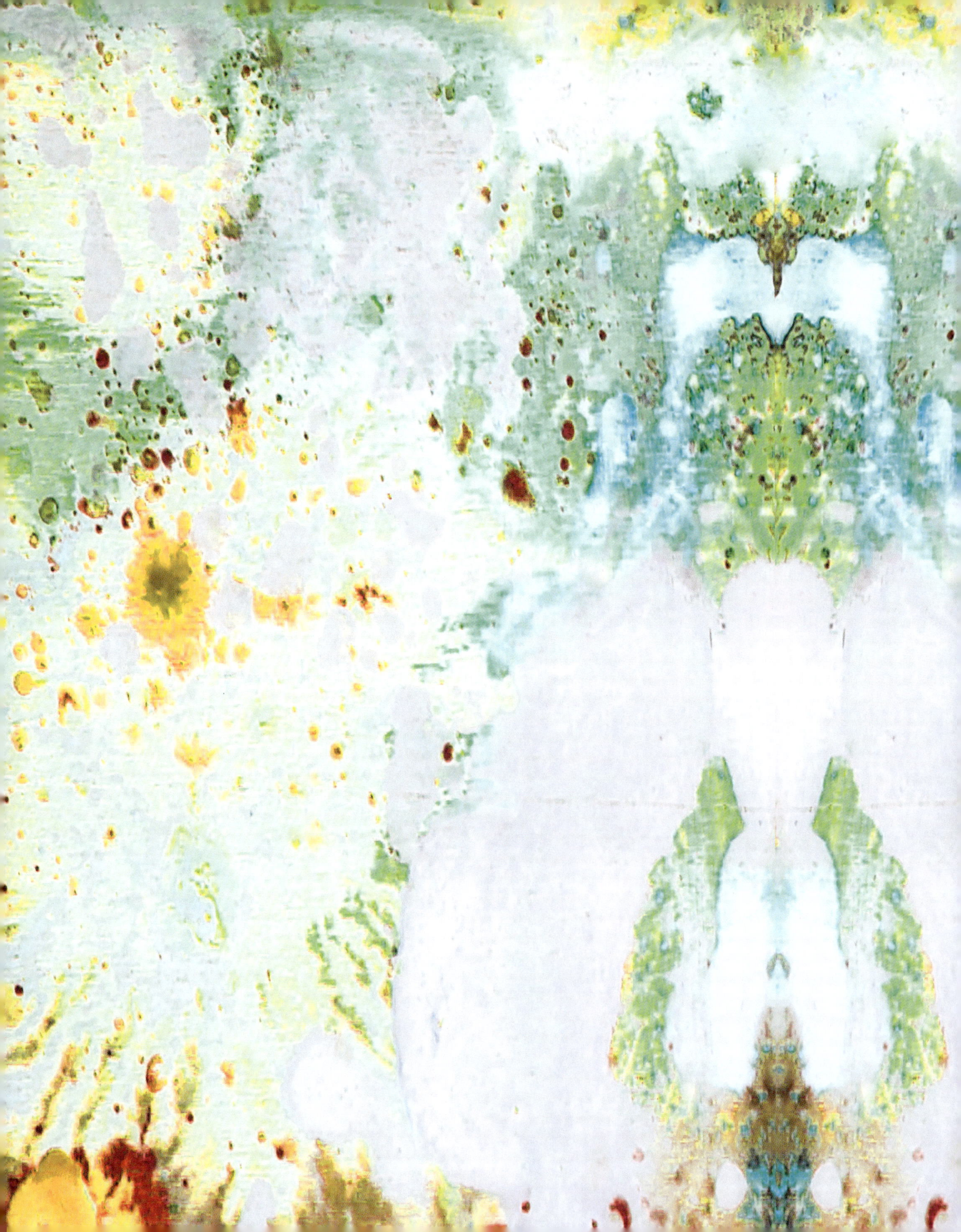

DEPTHS
MIKE LADD

We created these contraptions to summon you
Summon all the unsung beneath the seas and oceans

We built sub-bass to access a fortress in the low
A door to a refuge, our free, righteous watery end

The ocean, where bones roll, a seahorse clicks its skull
800 Hz, whale moan as slow as 25, who jumped

From ship decks, Guadeloupe cliffs, ramparts of sea forts
Into the terrible blue—Bosom of Olókun

We needed a sound system to conceive a sorrow that deep
Anchaing leapt from a peak on Reunion Island,

Say he flew, The Indian Ocean holding his wail
So many others' within The SOFAR Channel

A 1960 underwater bomb resonated from Australia to Bermuda
A gut punch thump of millions drowned, travels half that far

The Ocean, then China Seas to Osaka Bay
Makes sense Ikutaro Kakehashi could hear it

In his subconscious and invent the Roland 808
2SC828-R transistor deemed defective

Used from Detroit to Kingston rhythms
Effectively entrancing the world

Now they know the frequency of our humanity
But our audience was you, our aquatic marrow

Sine waves to oscillate for Ormerod
Sanite Bélair, Joseph Ignace and Toya

Claire the Maroon, we sew sonic waves to call you
From Atlantic fathoms deep, up the Amazon

Black Jacobin, scratch of your quill is air in a kick
The gasp in a woofer before it recedes

Cécile, Dutty, we send waves to Bois Caïman
To learn your physics of lambskin and wood

Soldering a tapestry of currents pulsing to a hum
Winding up transformers in homage to heroes ◆

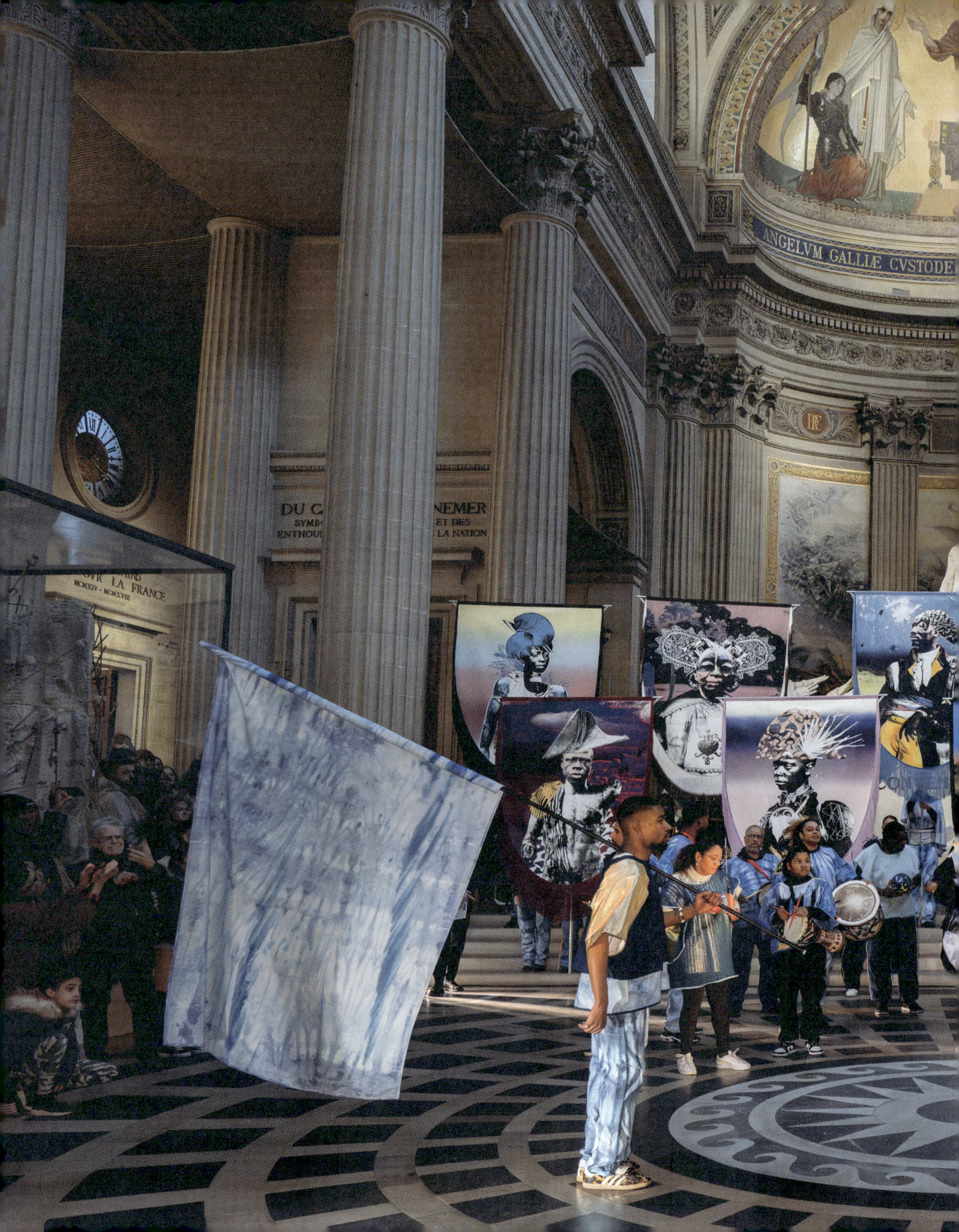
ANGELVM GALLIÆ CVSTODE
LA NATION
LA FRANCE
MCMXIV · MCMXVIII

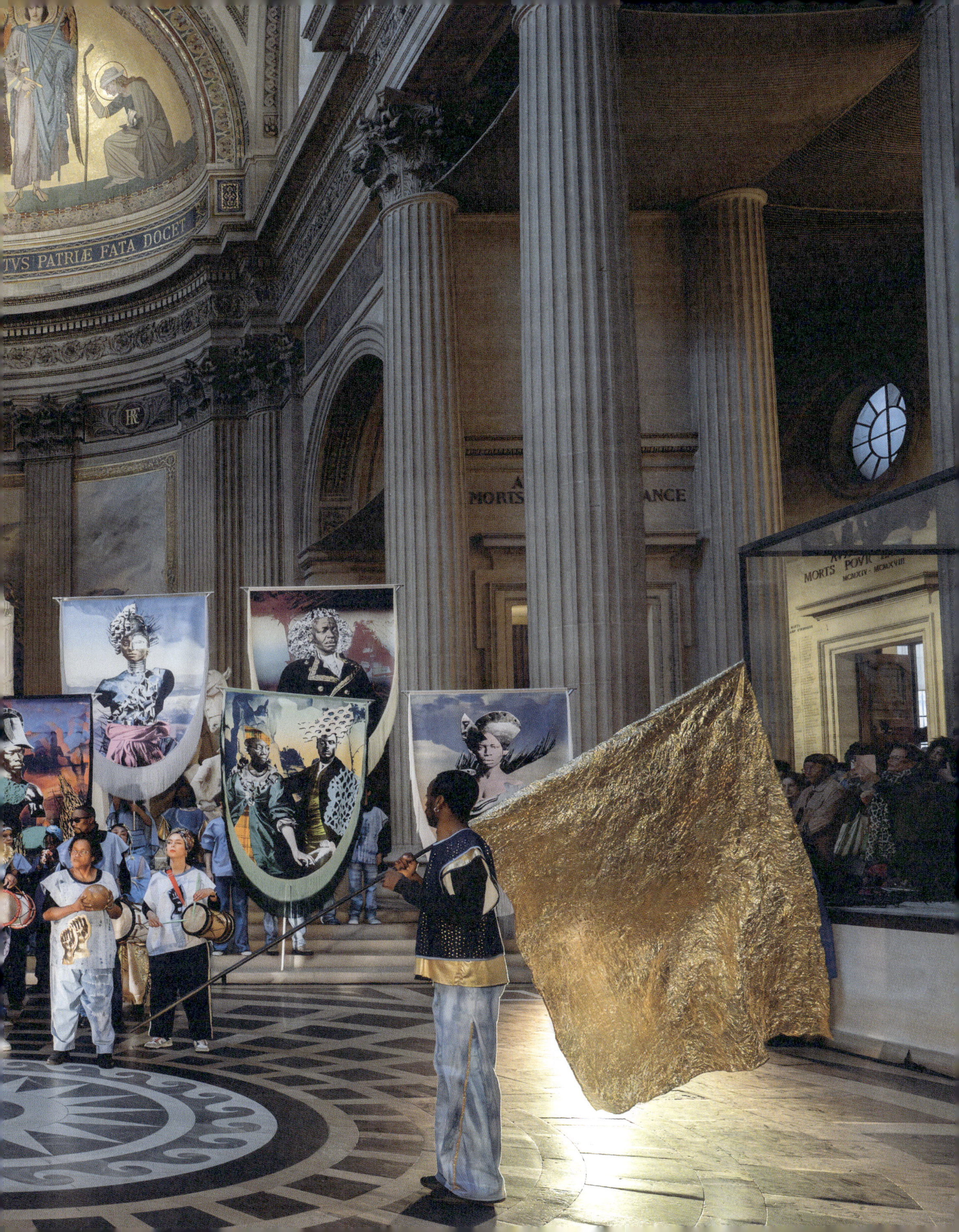
TVS PATRIÆ FATA DOCET

p. 92-93, 95-97, 99 Performance as part of the “We Could Be Heroes” exhibition, Panthéon, Paris, 2023

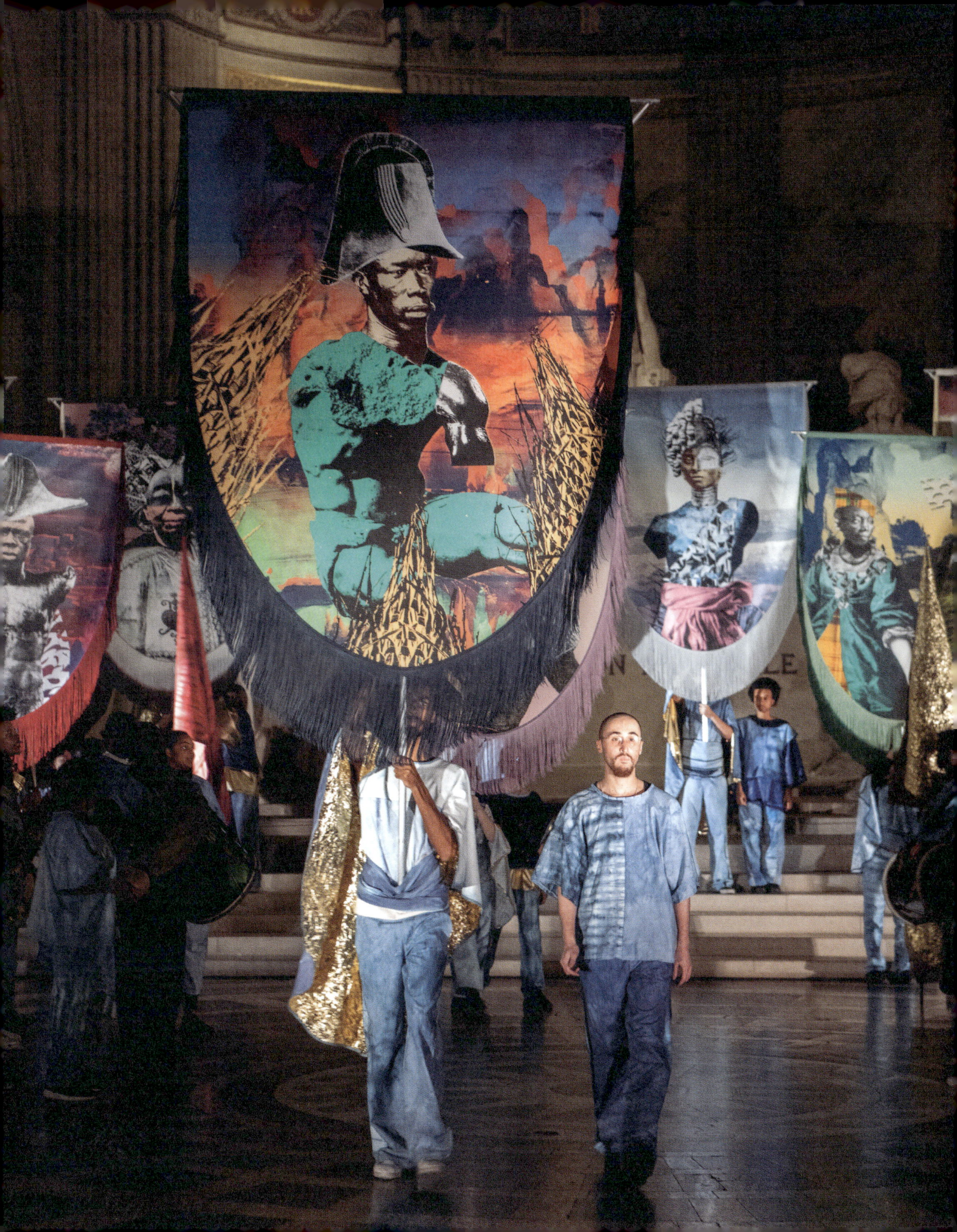

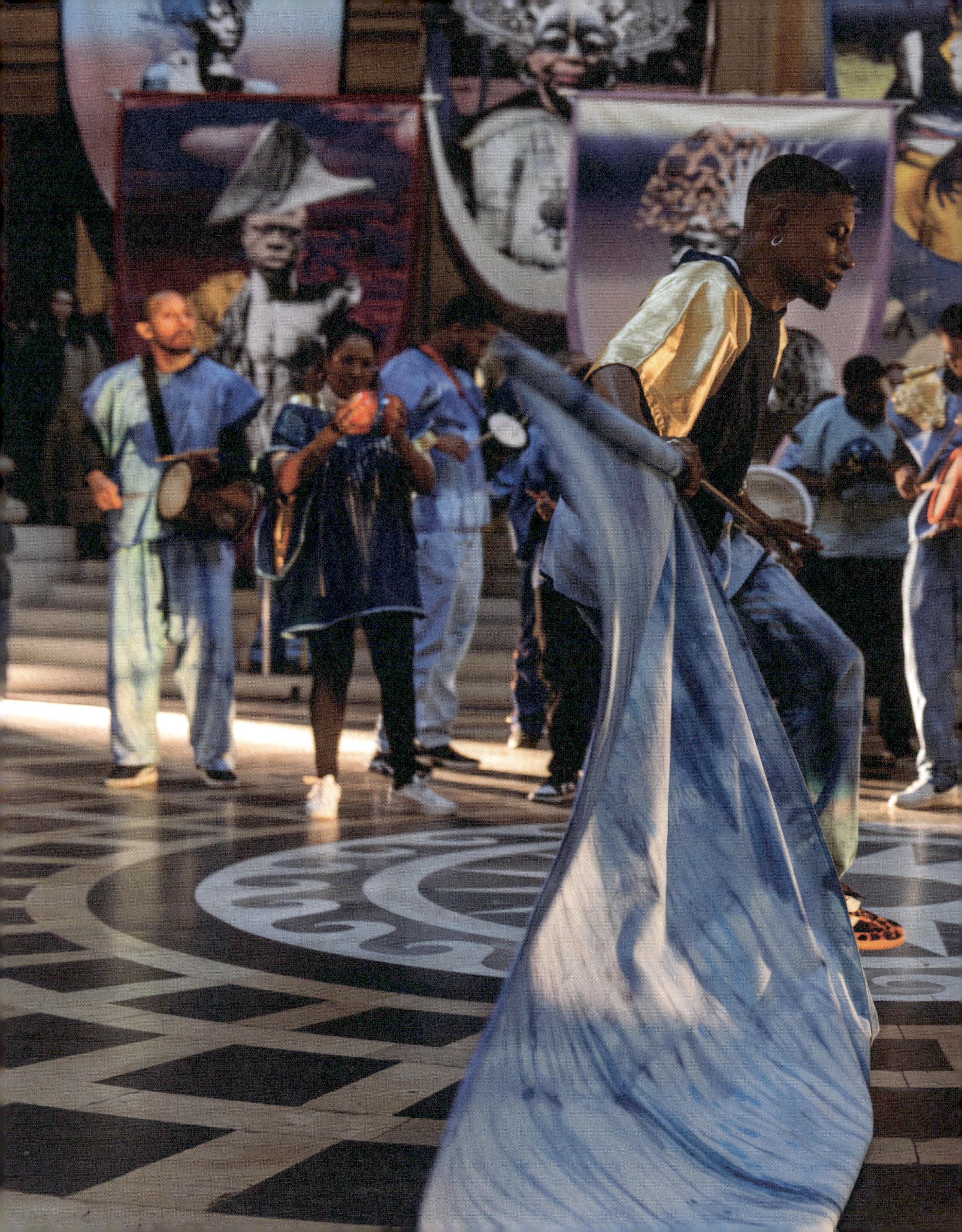

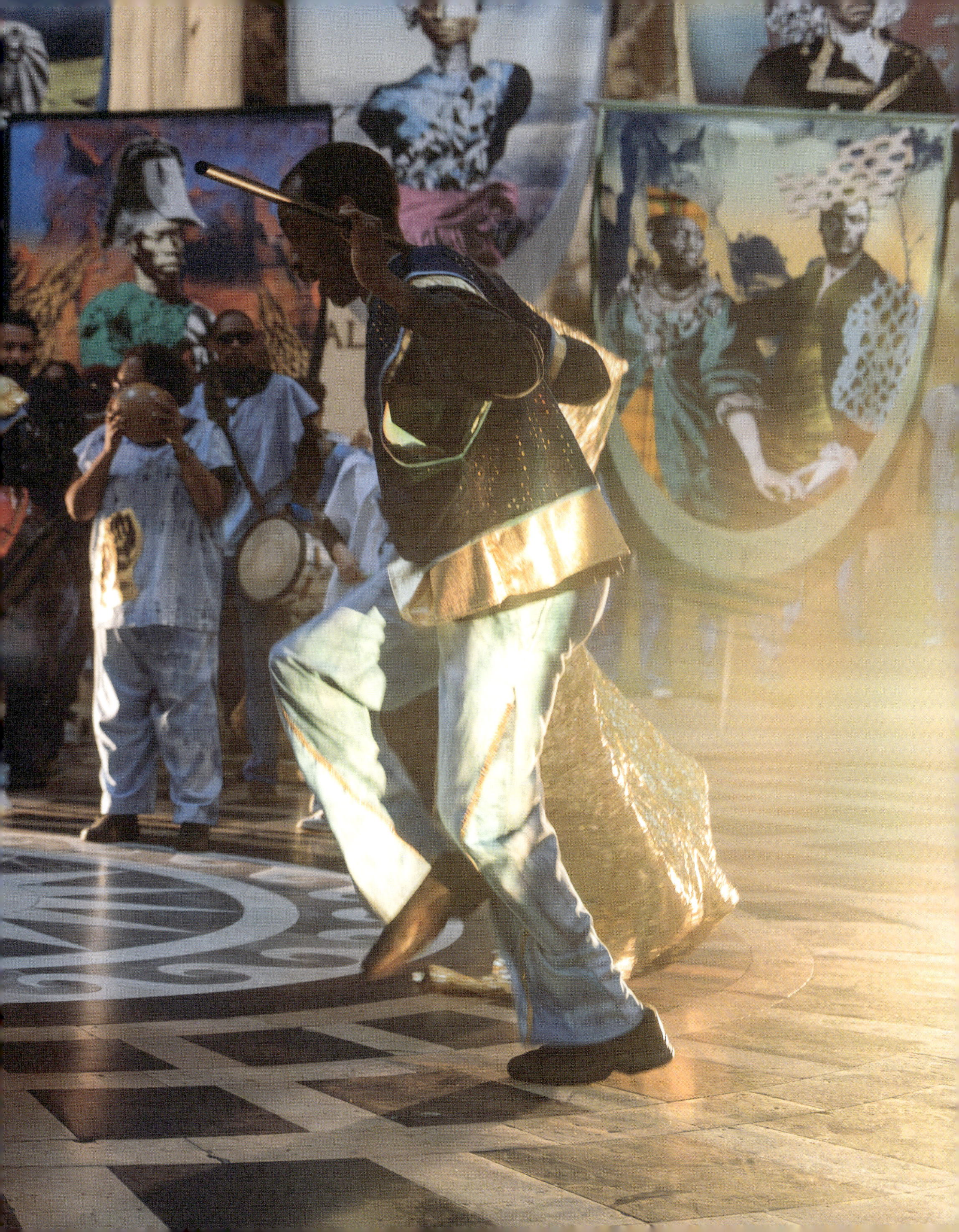

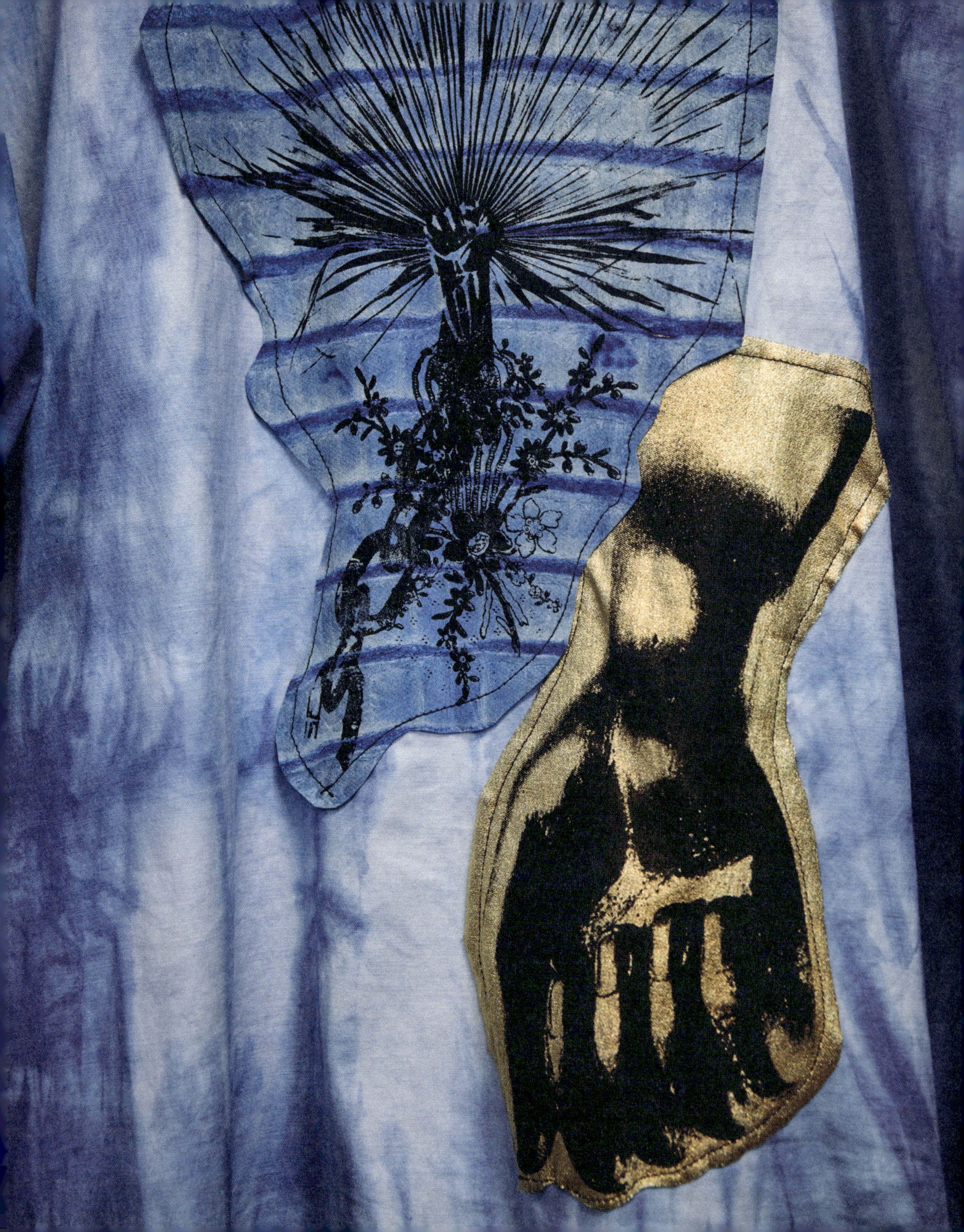

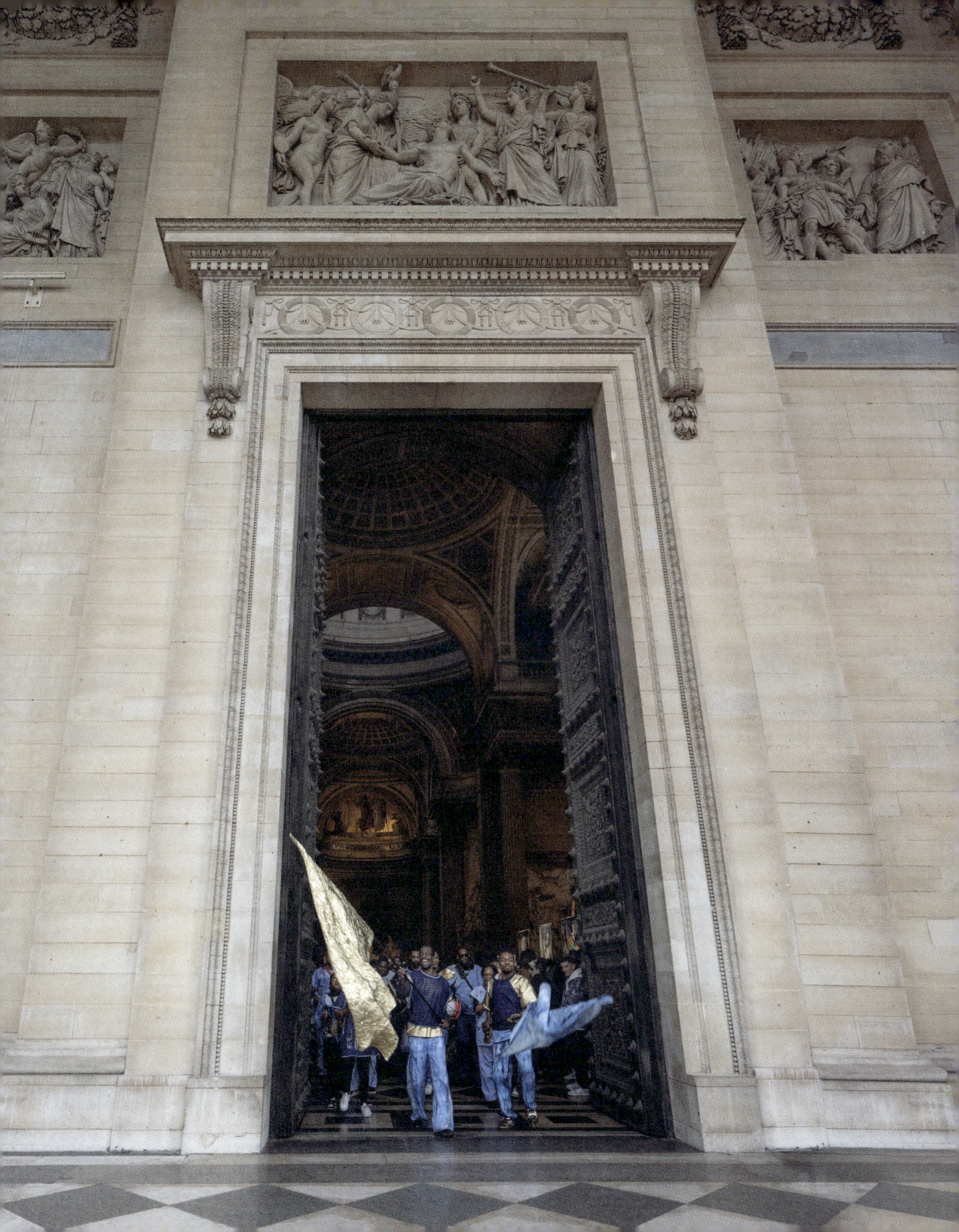

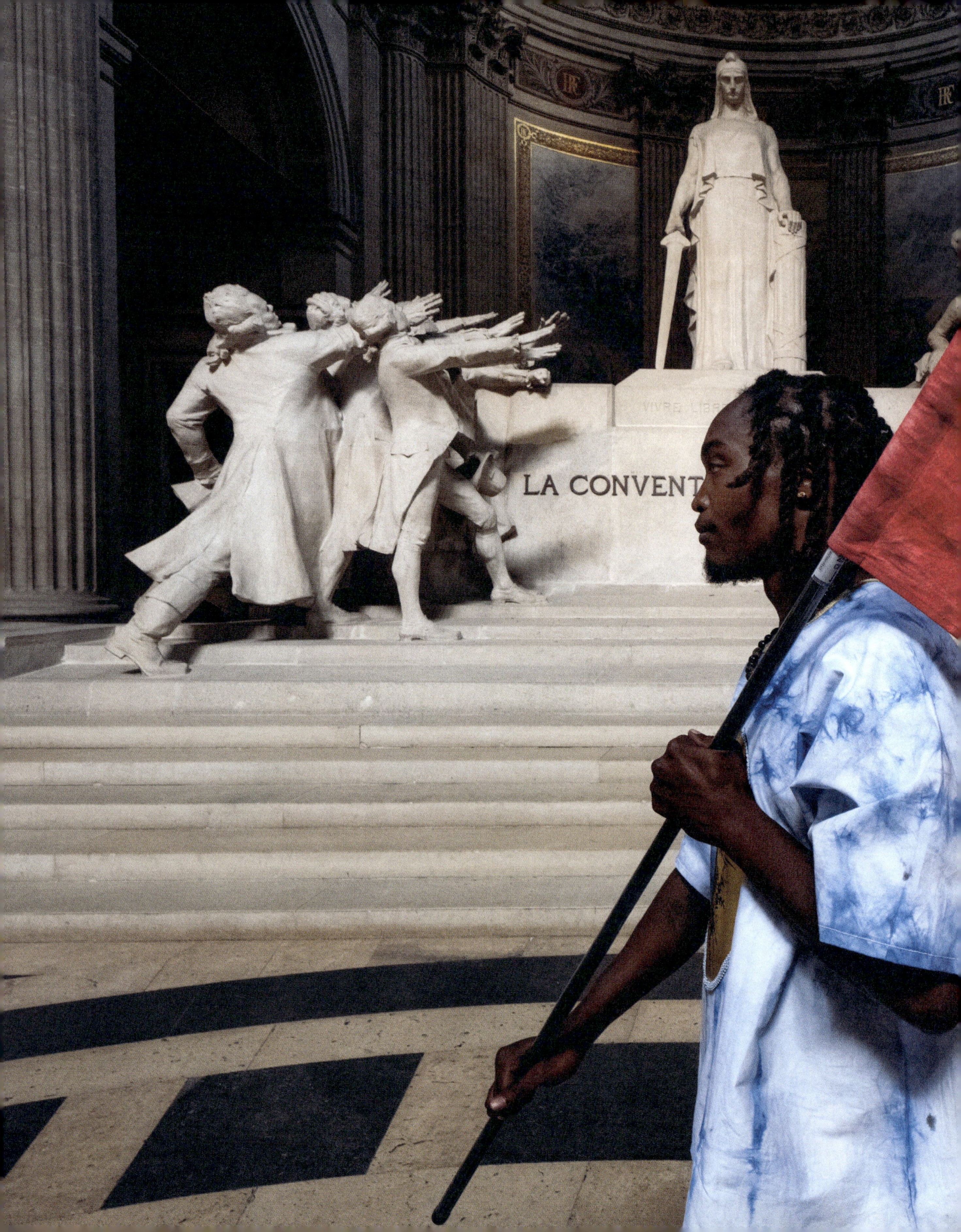
LA CONVENT

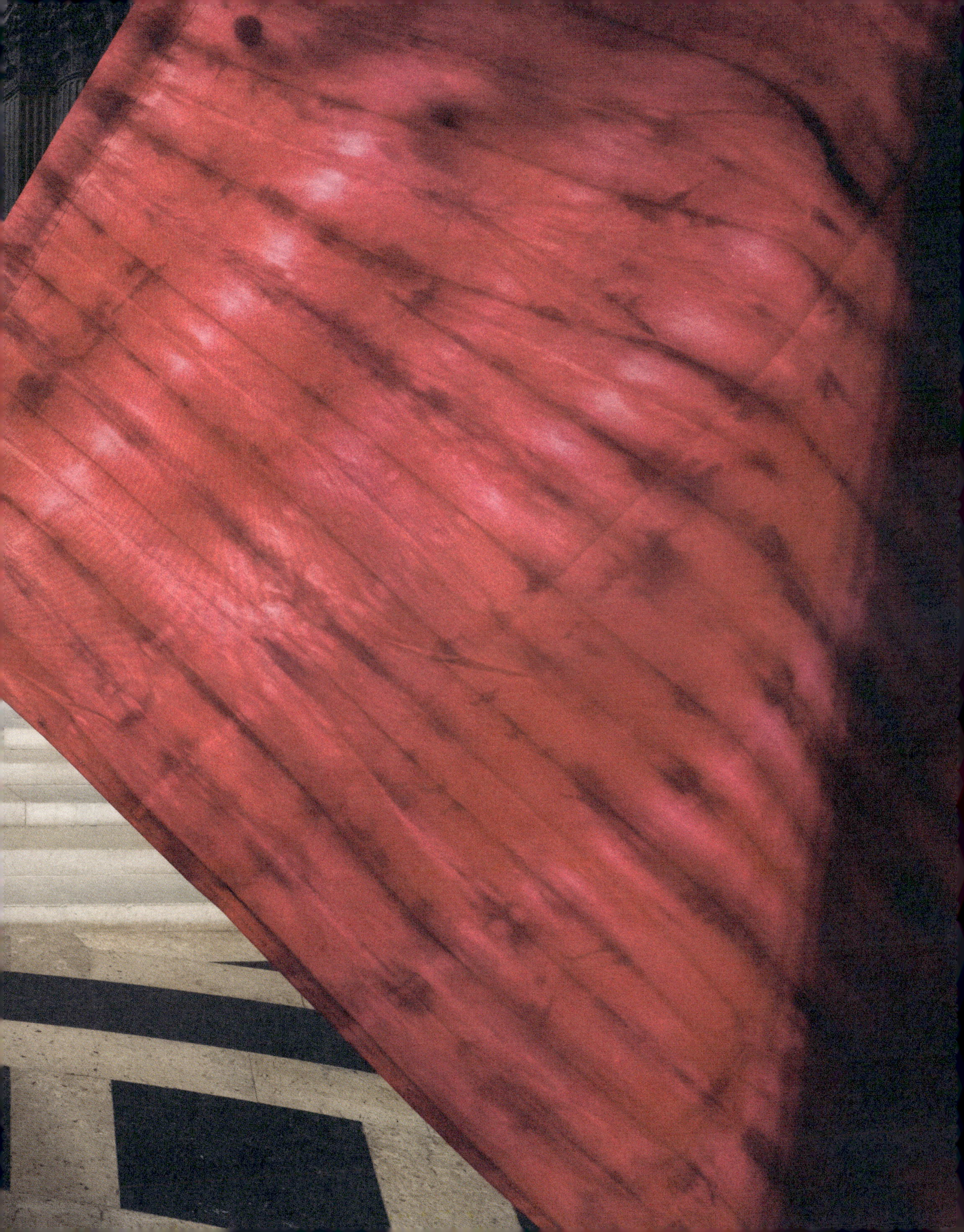

BANNERS

Acrylic, ink, silkscreen on canvas, dyed cotton lining, trimmings, aluminum pyramidal base
311 × 180 × 35 cm
2023

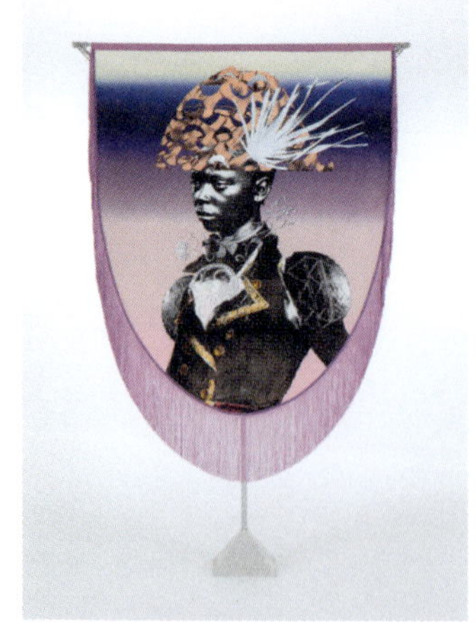

SANITÉ BÉLAIR

Sanite Bélair (c. 1781–1802) was born into slavery in Saint-Domingue. Once free she became a revolutionary, playing a major role in the confrontations that led to independence for Haiti by fighting General Leclerc's troops sent by Napoleon Bonaparte in 1802 to regain control of Saint-Domingue. Since the bicentenary of Haiti's independence in 2004, Sanite Bélair's portrait has been printed on Haitian ten gourd notes.

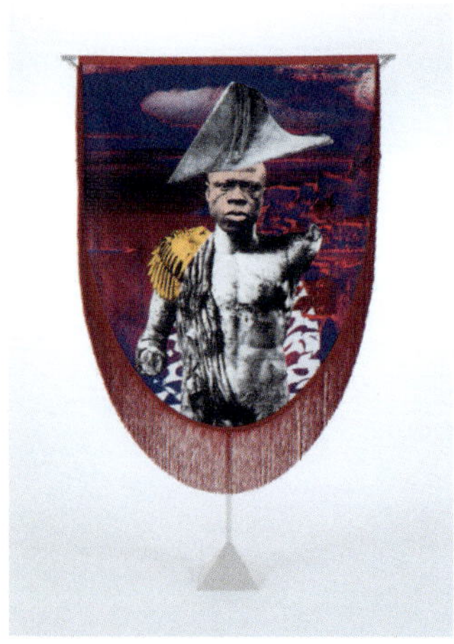

VOODOO MARCH – DUTTY BOUKMAN

Dutty Boukman (1767–1791) is one of the iconic figures of the August 1791 uprising in Saint-Domingue, which marked the beginning of the Haitian revolution. On the night of August 14-15, 1791 as a Voodoo priest, he led a ceremony at Bois Caïman, preparing the enslaved people in northern Saint-Domingue for the revolution, which erupted in 1794 and resulted in Haiti gaining independence in 1804.

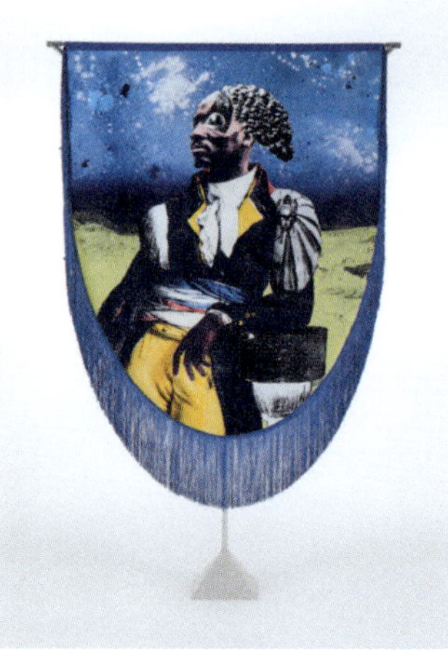

THE BLACK JACOBIN

Jean-Baptiste Belley (1746–1805) was the first ever Black deputy in the history of France. Elected in 1793 to represent Saint-Domingue in Paris, he was present at the national convention on February 4, 1794 when the first act abolishing slavery in all French colonies was voted into effect. As the spokesperson for the Black and multiracial populations of the French colonies, he symbolises all the struggles for equality undertaken by French citizens, regardless of their origin or the color of their skin.

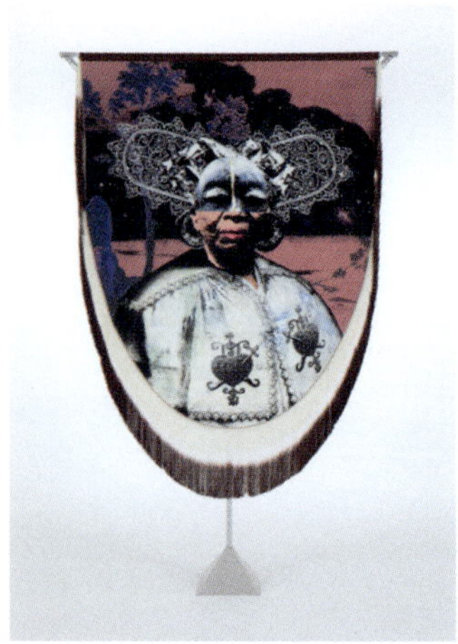

THE MAMBO OF BOIS-CAÏMAN – CÉCILE FATIMAN

Cécile Fatiman (1771–1883) was one of the many women who strove to achieve independence for the future Haiti. This Haitian Voodoo priestess played a crucial part in the Bois Caïman ceremony. She sacrificed a pig and offered its blood to the participants to give the rebels strength and courage for them to seal their oath to revolt. Her white tunic and the lace on her headdress recall the costumes worn by *mambos*, priestesses who interpreted the will of the spirits. On the upper part of her face can be seen a fragment of a *fon* fetish from present-day Benin, the birthplace of Voodoo.

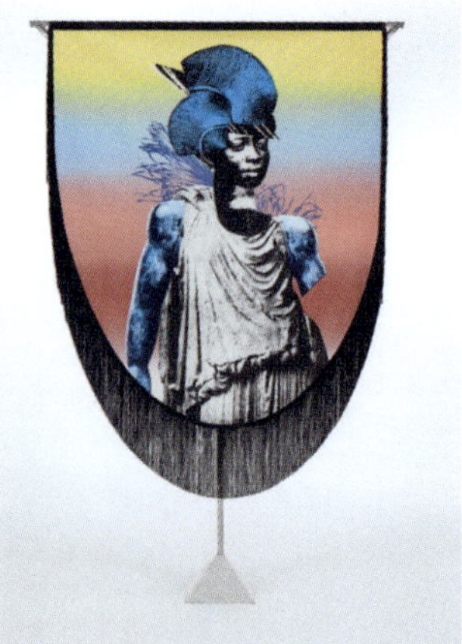

ORMEROD

Flore "Bois" Gaillard was born enslaved on the island of Saint-Lucia, located to the south of Martinique and at the time an object of dispute between France and England. In 1793, she became the main leader of the "*Armée française des bois*" [French Army of the Forest], which was made up of Maroons, free people of color and deserters from the French and English armies, who were all fighting the British troops sent to take back control of the island. Piton Flore, a mountain on the island of Saint Lucia, is named after her. She is also the hero of Edouard Glissant's 2003 novel, *Ormerod*.

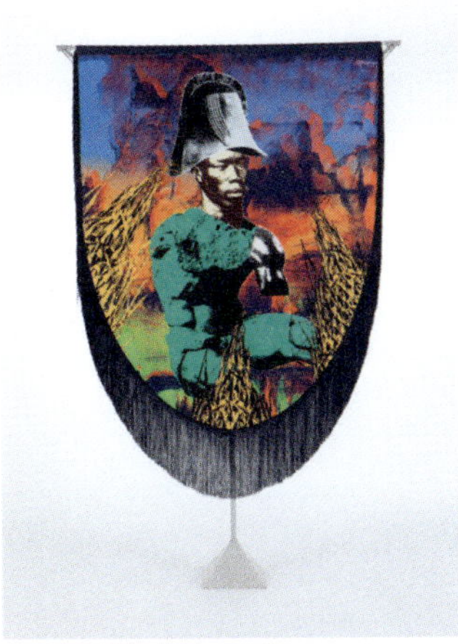

JOSEPH IGNACE

Joseph Ignace (1770–1802) was one of Gaudeloupe's first insurgents, in 1802. He became the leader of one of the battalions confronting General Richepanse's troops, sent by Napoleon Bonaparte to re-establish slavery. Like Louis Delgrès, he preferred to commit suicide rather than give up the fight for freedom.

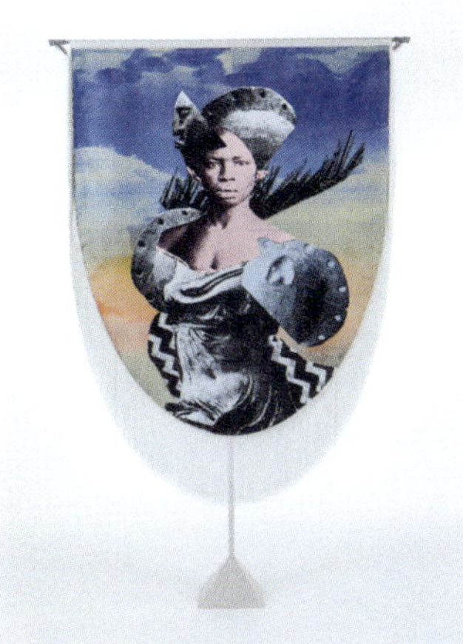

TOYA

Victoria Montou (mid 18th century–1805), aka "Toya," was born in the Kingdom of Dahomey (present-day Benin) where she learned the fighting techniques that made her famous. Captured and enslaved, she was deported to Saint-Domingue, where she became friendly with the future emperor of Haiti, Jean-Jacques Dessalines.

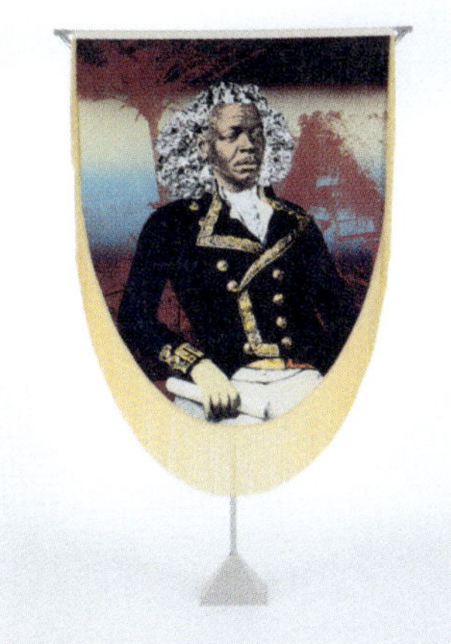

TO THE WHOLE UNIVERSE, THE LAST CRY OF INNOCENCE AND DESPAIR. – LOUIS DELGRÈS

"Live free or die" was the motto guiding the actions of Louis Delgrès (1766–1802). He was in command of the revolts that took place in Guadeloupe in 1802 against the reintroduction of slavery, ordered by Napoleon Bonaparte, and chose to commit suicide alongside three hundred of his men rather than surrender to the French army. The letter that Louis Delgrès is holding in his right hand references the Proclamation he made in 1802, which begins: "*The last cry of innocence and despair. It is in the brightest days of a century that shall forever be known for the triumph of the Enlightenment and of philosophy, that a class of unfortunate souls whom some wish to crush, find themselves forced to raise their voices towards posterity, so that when they have vanished, posterity may know of their innocence and misfortunes.*"

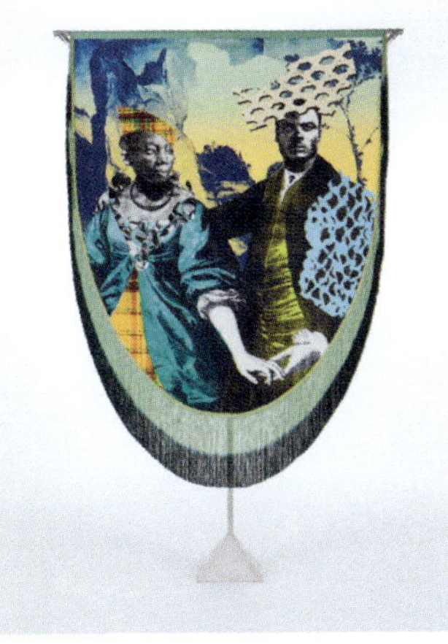

ANCHAING & HÉVA

Blurring the lines between myth and reality, the story of Anchaing and Héva, a Maroon couple said to have lived in the colony of the Isle of Bourbon, now Reunion Island, embodies the plans and acts of resistance of the Maroon communities that developed in the island's inland valleys, or cirques. One of the peaks in the Cirque of Salazie, where the couple took refuge, is now known as the Piton of Anchaing.

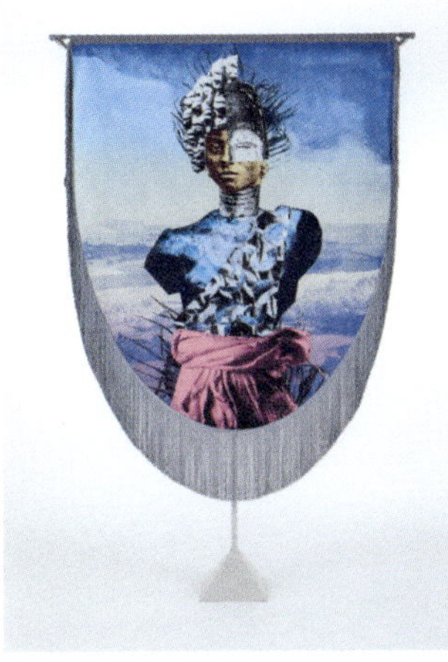

CLAIRE, THE MAROON FROM MONTAGNE PLOMB

Claire (1700–1752) symbolises the history of the Maroons in French Guiana. Helped by the Amazonian environment, Guiana's enslaved population formed their own counter societies in the heart of the forest, making a living from farming, hunting and fishing. Claire ran away from the plantation and joined the Maroon community on Montagne-Plomb, which had been resisting attacks from the French army since 1742. Captured and hanged in 1752, she, along with the many other women who were in Maroon camps at the time, was the embodiment of the motto "Live free or die."

NORTH TRANSEPT

Silkscreen print on fabric,
digital print on fabric, dyed cotton
Variable dimensions
2023

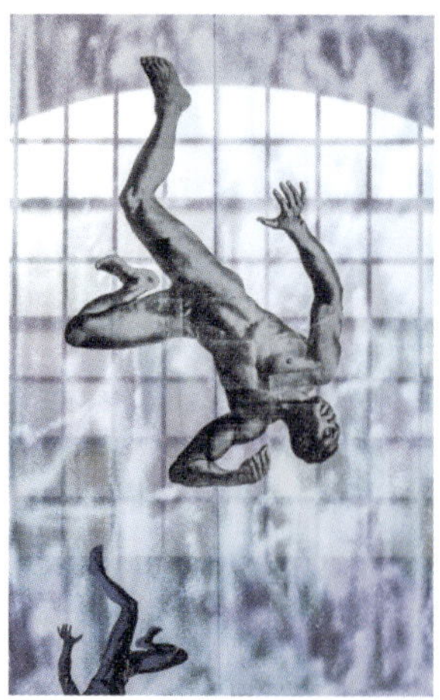

THE ABYSS

The Abyss is a metaphorical reference to falling into the abyss of slavery. Innumerable enslaved people lost their lives on the deportation to the Americas owing to the inhuman conditions of transport in the holds of these ships: their deaths were a result of suicide, insurrection and disease. The person seen falling is Joseph, a famous 19th century Black artist's model. First painted by Théodore Chassériau, he was also immortalized by the artists Jacques-Louis David and Théodore Géricault.

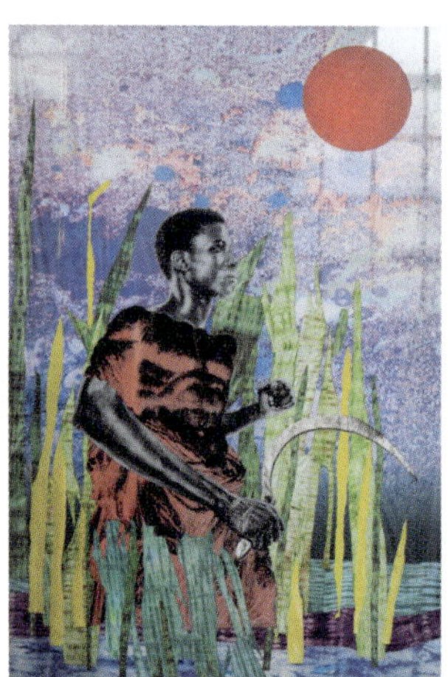

THE MAROON

The Maroon pays homage to the anonymous masses of enslaved people who tried to escape their servitude. From the hills and mountains of Guadeloupe and Reunion Island to the Amazonian forests of Guiana, these fugitives were the first heroes of the resistance against slavery.

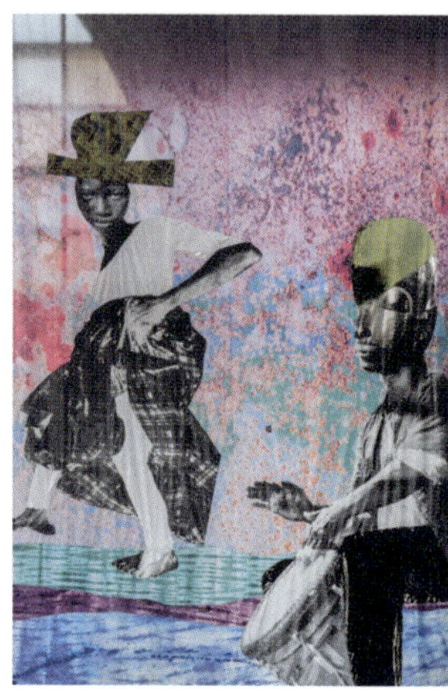

LÉWOZ

Léwoz speaks of the music and dance traditions that developed on the plantations of Guadeloupe and Martinique. Léwoz is a traditional artistic act involving singing and percussion ("Ka") that first appeared on the plantations.

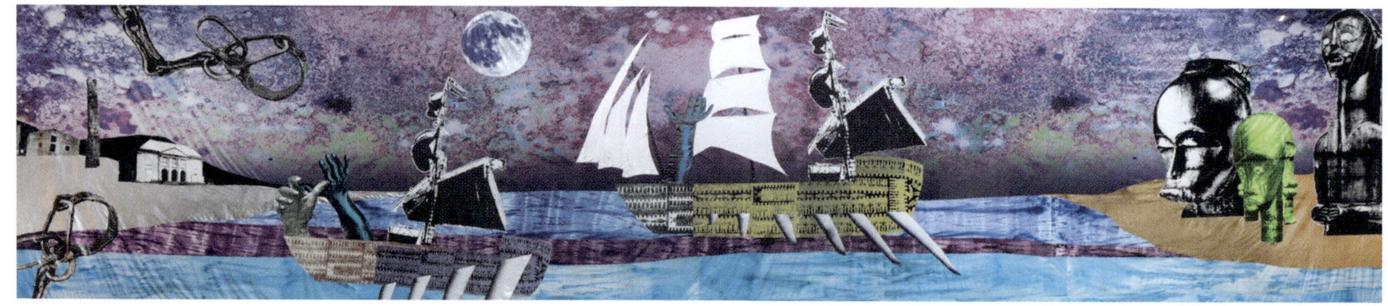

THE CROSSING

The largest of the works presented here speaks of the slave trade as one facet of triangular trade, in which millions of men and women were uprooted from the African continent, deported across the Atlantic ocean and enslaved. To the left of the work is shown one of Guadeloupe's oldest plantations, in Marie Galante.

SOUTH TRANSEPT

Silkscreen print on fabric,
digital print on fabric, dyed cotton
Variable dimensions
2023

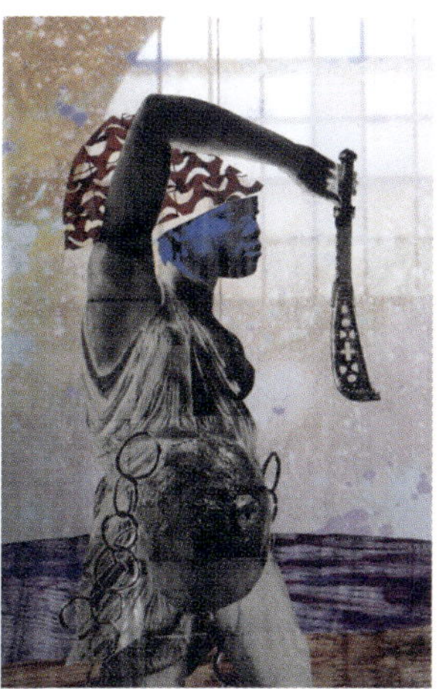

SOLITUDE

In 1802, Solitude (c. 1772–1802), a historical figure who later became the hero of a novel by André Schwarz-Bart, fought Napoleon's troops despite her pregnancy. Arrested and imprisoned, her execution was set for the day after she had given birth. A few months later, slavery would be established on the island once again. Solitude is an iconic figure of the resistance in Guadeloupe.

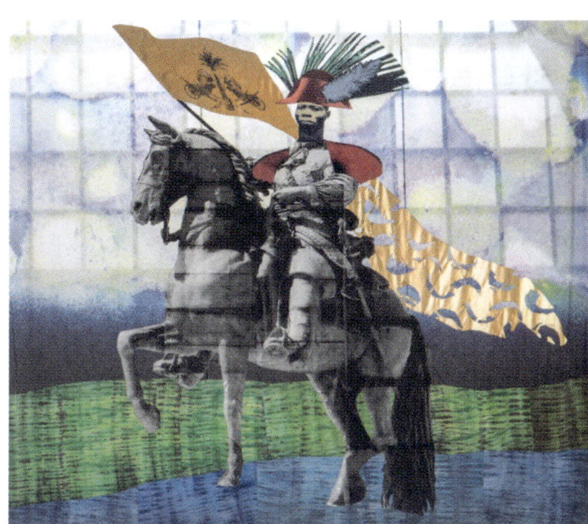

TOUSSAINT'S TRIUMPH

Toussaint Louverture (1743–1803) is a hero of Haitian revolution and the fight to abolish slavery. Born on the Bréda plantation in Saint-Domingue, in 1776 he was emancipated, and, after the abolition of slavery in the colonies, he fought alongside the French to achieve independence for the island from Spain. In 1801, he had a constitution adopted appointing him governor for life. The following year, he resisted General Leclerc's troops sent by the First Consul Bonaparte to overthrow him. Defeated, he was arrested by surprise and deported to Fort de Joux in the Jura mountains, where he died alone in 1803, nine months before Haiti's independence.

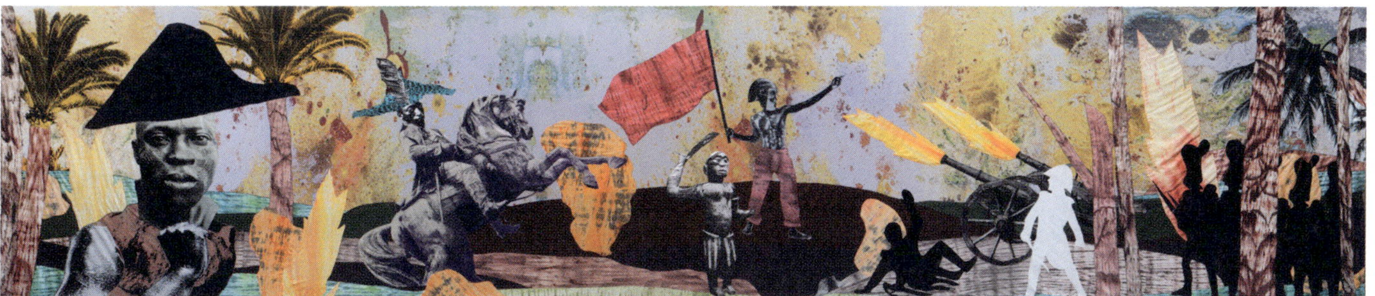

THE BATTLE OF VERTIÈRES

The Battle of Vertières (November 18, 1803) was a decisive turning point for Haitian independence, in that the rebels defeated Napoleon's troops, thereby paving the way for Haiti to become the first Black Republic in 1804. Haiti was the only French colony in the Caribbean, to achieve independence through armed insurrection.

CREDITS

P 4, 13-14
© Photo: Claire Delannoy
Courtesy Raphaël Barontini and Mouhameth Ndiaye

P 16
Beinecke Rare Book and Manuscript Library

P 18
© Montauban, musée Ingres Bourdelle / Photo: Guy Roumagnac

P 21
© Musée du quai Branly - Jacques Chirac, Dist. GrandPalaisRmn / picture musée Guimet

P 21
Artwork © Kara Walker, courtesy of Sikkema Jenkins & Co. and Sprüth Magers
Installation view: Kara Walker: My Complement, My Enemy, My Oppressor,
My Love Hammer Museum, Los Angeles, 2008
Photo: Joshua White

P 28-29, 55, 56-57, 74-75, 77
Exhibition view "We Could Be Heroes", Panthéon, Paris (FR), 2023
Commissioned by the Centre des monuments nationaux - Panthéon
© Photo: Benjamin Gavaudo / Centre des monuments nationaux
Courtesy Raphaël Barontini and Mariane Ibrahim, Chicago, Paris, Mexico City

P 30-31, 33, 34, 37, 41, 43, 45, 46-47, 51, 60-61, 63, 64, 67, 69, 71, 73, 78-79, 83, 89, 104, 105
Exhibition view "We Could Be Heroes", Panthéon, Paris (FR), 2023
Commissioned by the Centre des monuments nationaux - Panthéon
© Photo: Fabrice Gousset
Courtesy Raphaël Barontini and Mariane Ibrahim, Chicago, Paris, Mexico City

P 35, 36, 38-39, 40, 52-53, 58-59, 62, 65, 66, 70, 84-85, 86-87, 100-101
© Photo: Fabrice Gousset
Courtesy Raphaël Barontini and Mariane Ibrahim, Chicago, Paris, Mexico City

P 49, 81
© Photo: Benjamin Gavaudo / Centre des monuments nationaux
Courtesy Raphaël Barontini and Mariane Ibrahim, Chicago, Paris, Mexico City

P 90
Courtesy Raphaël Barontini

P 92-93, 95, 99
Panthéon, Paris (FR), 2023
© Photo: Fabrice Gousset
Courtesy Raphaël Barontini and Mariane Ibrahim, Chicago, Paris, Mexico City

P 96-97
Panthéon, Paris (FR), 2023
© Photo: Willy Vainqueur
Courtesy Raphaël Barontini and Mariane Ibrahim, Chicago, Paris, Mexico City

P 98
© Photo: Claire Delannoy
Courtesy Raphaël Barontini and École Duperré Paris

P 102-103
© Photo: Claire Delannoy
Courtesy Raphaël Barontini and Mariane Ibrahim, Chicago, Paris, Mexico City

P 109
© Photo: Jalil Ourguedi
Courtesy Raphaël Barontini and Mariane Ibrahim, Chicago, Paris, Mexico City

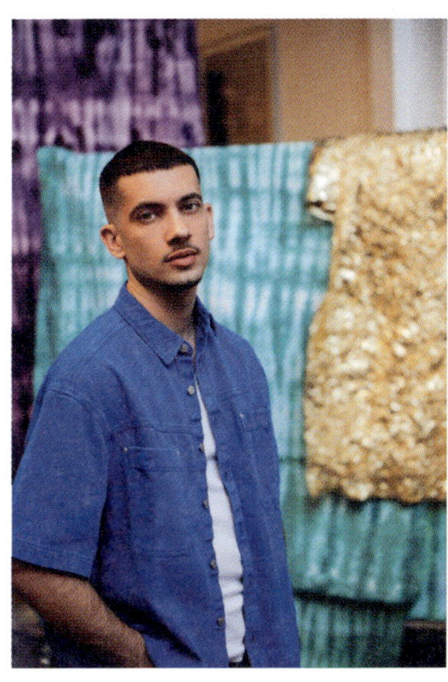

RAPHAËL BARONTINI

Raphaël Barontini was born in 1984 in Saint-Denis, France. He lives and works in Saint-Denis. Barontini's combination of silkscreen printing, painting, and digital printing results in a style of painting in movement that offers a new perspective on history, whilst simultaneously asking questions about the very status of painting in a museum or public space.
Raphaël Barontini's work has been exhibited in international institutions, including Panthéon, Paris (FR); SCAD Museum of Art, Savannah (USA); Currier Museum of Art, Manchester (USA); New Art Exchange Museum, Nottingham (RU); Museum of African Diaspora, San Francisco (USA); MAC VAL, Vitry-sur-Seine (FR); MO.CO Montpellier (FR); Louvre-Lens, Lens (FR); Museum of Arts and Design, New York (USA).
He is represented by Mariane Ibrahim (Chicago, Paris, Mexico City).

PATRICK CHAMOISEAU

Patrick Chamoiseau was born in Fort-de-France (France) in 1953. Poet, novelist and essayist, his work has been widely acclaimed (Carbet de la Caraïbe prize, Goncourt prize, Marguerite Yourcenar prize, etc.) and translated worldwide. His aesthetic explores the creolization and relational poetics of the contemporary world. Today, he is one of the most important literary figures in the Caribbean.

CHERYL FINLEY

Cheryl Finley, Ph.D., is an American-born art historian, author, curator and critic. Committed to the transformation of the art and culture industry, she directs an innovative program designed to prepare the next generation of African American museum and visual arts leaders. She won Bard Graduate Center's Horowitz Book Prize (2019) and Howard University's James A. Porter Book Prize (2023) for *Committed to Memory: The Art of the Slave Ship Icon* (Princeton University Press, 2018).

MIKE LADD

Michael (Mike) Ladd was born in Boston (USA) in 1970. He is a Black American poet, lyricist and music creator. He has released over fourteen records with important labels. He has created soundtracks for Netflix series, short films and soundscapes for artists Kanishka Raja and Barontini. He's performed his original work worldwide including The Metropolitan Museum of Art (NYC), Queen Elizabeth Hall and L'Olympia in Paris. His writing has appeared in numerous literary magazines and anthologies including *Long Shot Review* and *Bostonia*.

At the Panthéon, the Centre des Monuments Nationaux has dedicated an exhibition to artist Raphaël Barontini in the form of a carte blanche. In this place of memory of the greatness of republican commitment, where the echoes of the battles against slavery—those of Condorcet, Louverture and Schœlcher, among many others—resonate, the artist proposed his "imaginary Panthéon". It is populated by the powerful faces of men and women who rose up against slavery to defend freedom in the West Indies, French Guiana and Reunion Island. It is nourished by tales of terror and downfall, battle scenes and victories, in dialogue with the great historical paintings in the Panthéon. Inviting artists to the Panthéon is nothing new. Visual artists Sarkis, Ernesto Neto, Gérard Garouste, JR and Ann Veronica Janssens, as well as choreographers Carolyn Carlson, Radhouane El Meddeb, Yoann Bourgeois, Nacera Belaza and Faustin Linyekula, have already presented their work there. These dialogues with the architecture, décor, history and memories of the Panthéon, which also regularly take the form of readings or ceremonies to grant French nationality, are all opportunities to highlight one of the many aspects of the monument and to open up to new audiences. For the Panthéon is plural: in its history and its uses, in the debates that run through it, in the infinite richness of the commitments of the great men and women who inhabit it, and in its role in the service of society as a whole.
There is no doubt that this carte blanche for Raphaël Barontini—which was part of the wider "Dare to be Free" exhibition, retracing the history of the fight against slavery—has once again contributed to making the Panthéon a lively and vibrant place.

Marie Lavandier
President, Centre des Monuments Nationaux

CENTRE DES MONUMENTS NATIONAUX

President
Marie Lavandier

Managing Director
Delphine Samsœn

Director of Cultural Development and Visitors
Edward de Lumley

Head of Cultural Events Department
Anne-Isabelle Vignaud

Exhibition Project Manager
Julie Delacotte assistée de Roxane Michoud

Head of Administrative and Financial Management
Dominique Amri-Goldschneider

Head of Communications
Delphine Jeammet

And all the teams at the Centre des Monuments Nationaux head office

PANTHÉON

Administrator
Barbara Wolffer

Cultural Action Officer
Édouard Bueno

Education Officer
Mathilde Garnier

Communications Officer
Mégane Thellier

Booking and Visitor Development Manager
Alex Le Gad

And the entire Panthéon team

STUDIO RAPHAËL BARONTINI

Studio Manager
Muriel Babandisha

Studio team
Manon Aniambossou, Alexandre Bouphavichith, Te Ata Hapaitahaa Conroy, Salomé Henry, Aurore Maisondieu, Jalil Ourguedi, Rim Sli, Nathanaël Tardy, Maxime Toutain, Elijah Verrier, Jenifer Zako

PRODUCTION

Joinery
Julie Stockmann

Ironwork
Boucan Oiseau - Walter Bilirit

Installation of the works
Coopérative Octopus

Lighting design
Studio 10-30 - Léopold Mauger

Lighting
Transpalux

Graphics
Antoine Caquard

Mediation coordination
Éléonore Gros

Printing
Opéra Print

Video
Fabien Mariano Ortiz,
art/beats (Felix von Boehm)

Exhibition presentation text
Humberto Moro

Mediation texts
Manon Aniambossou, Raphaël Barontini

Translation
Traducteo

COSTUMES WORKSHOP ÉCOLE DUPERRÉ

Principal
Alain Soreil

Public Relations Manager
Étienne Périn

Teachers
Mathieu Buard, Thom Friedlander, Céline Mallet

Students
Naomi Berry, Swann Bossé, Violette Chanel-Valla, Olympe Deboaisne, Marceline Hebert, Chloé Hubert, Eliot Jeanjean, Femi Kinkingnehun, Anna Krasnoshapka, Aurélien Lefebvre, Angelina Mourrat and Sarah Philippe-Picard, May De Sousa, Charlotte Donnay, Zoé Douay, Coline Falk, Maya Katz, Enza Morvant, Mélanie Reis Neves, Anjela Rubin, Kali Thommes

WE COULD BE HEROES

Head of publishing
David Desrimais

Editing
Raphaël Barontini with Muriel Babandisha
David Desrimais with Lisa Valentin

Index texts
Manon Aniambossou

Translation and proofreading
Cassandra Katsiaficas

Graphic design
Emma Zampieri — Studio JBE

Photographers
Claire Delannoy
Benjamin Gavaudo
Fabrice Gousset
Willy Vainqueur

Photoengraving
IGS-Print

Typefaces
Industry (Fort Foundry)
Spectral (Production Type)

The artist would like to thank in particular:
Marie Lavandier, Pierre Bélaval, Edward de Lumley, Barbara Wolffer, as well as the CMN teams and Henri van Melle.
Mariane Ibrahim and all the gallery teams.
The different contributors Patrick Chamoiseau, Cheryl Finley, Mike Ladd and Humberto Moro.
The different patrons Jacques-Antoine Granjon, Chargeurs Philanthropies, Stéphanie Fribourg, Éric Kayser, Fondation pour la mémoire de l'esclavage (the Foundation for the memory of slavery), Joachim Pflieger, Reuben O. Charles II.
Claire Delannoy, Mouhameth Ndiaye, Fabrice Gousset, Felix von Boehm and Art Beats.
Le Mas Choukaj, Didier Dorzille, Patrick Duport, Samuel Féréol, Lino Trepont, Thomas Radin, Yonas Perou, Andrège Bidiamambu, Florence Alexis, Claire Tancons, David Démétrius.
The students of École Duperré as well as Céline Mallet, Thom Friedlander and Mathieu Buard (teachers), Étienne Périn (public relations manager), Alain Soreil (principal).
ICART, Nicolas Laugero Lasserre.

JBE Books would like to thank in particular:
Aure Bergeret, Mathieu Cénac, Pierre-Édouard Couton, Benjamin Hélion, Mariane Ibrahim, Damien Jacq, Benjamin Lanot, Olivia de Smedt.

ISBN 978-2-36568-093-6
Legal deposit: November 2024
Printed in Lithuania

JBE Books
90 rue de la Folie-Méricourt
75011 Paris
jbe-books.com